"DIFFICULT
SCRIPTURES"

COVER DESIGN BY DICK JOHNS GRAFIX, TYLER, TEXAS

Coming to Grips with the Law of Moses
in the Worldwide Church of God

"DIFFICULT SCRIPTURES"

David Albert

TYLER HOUSE

**Attention colleges and universities, churches, and professional
organizations:** Quanitity discounts are available on bulk
purchases of this book for educational training purposes,
fund raising, or gift giving.
For information contact:
Tyler House, Box 132327, Tyler, Texas 75713

Acknowledgments

Without the help and support of the following people, "Difficult Scriptures" would never have gone to press:

Because of her long exposure to Worldwide Church of God literature, her *superb* editorial talents, and our warm friendship going back many years, Stephanie Vitale was, for me, the *perfect* editor. By always going the extra mile, she made what I feared might be a long and painful process, short, pleasant, and delightful. Thanks again, "Stephie-Ed." You're good at what you do!

Dee Archer was from the beginning eager to help with the desktop publishing and electronic typesetting—both of which I knew little or nothing about. She also made a considerable contribution to the interior layout and design. Her careful attention to a thousand details was a great help.

Jeff and Terrie Payne gave me emotional and prayerful support at every stage of the way, and Terrie's thorough proof reading was much needed on those *very* rough drafts. Every new author should be so lucky to have friends like you!

In many rich conversations, my good friend and fellow boat builder Jim Puntney helped me keep the focus on the needs of the reader. He also helped guide the book by simply living by the New Covenant of Jesus Christ. Jim, you sure have been there for me this past year. I'm convinced your coming into my life was a godsend.

Simone, thanks beyond words for being my best friend and my partner in life. Thank you for your kind and generous support of not one but two major projects—a boat and a book—in the same calendar year!

And to all of you who voiced your encouragement and sent up your prayers, thanks again. May our combined efforts be a blessing to many.

Foreword

In the past four or five years, thousands of members of the Worldwide Church of God have been impacted by the controversy and turmoil that have arisen as a result of far-reaching doctrinal changes. Friends and family members have left our fellowship to join other churches. It has been very painful and extremely traumatic.

On a personal level, I've had to deal with "the issues," and have also been wounded by the controversy. I'm deeply grateful that I now see our doctrinal re-focus as scriptural and foundational. Yet I can still identify with those who struggle because I have struggled, too.

In his book "Difficult Scriptures", Dave Albert provides a thoughtful and biblically-based analysis of the real issues inherent in the Old Covenant-New Covenant discussion. He explains, with much careful analysis, that our Church has been in error in its view of the Law of Moses. I deeply appreciate his vibrant call to recover from the Scriptures those paramount truths that can lead us into the light of the glorious Gospel of Jesus Christ. If you're still confused by doctrinal re-focus, "Difficult Scriptures" can change your life.

I recognize that it is tough to change ingrained, cherished beliefs. It is my prayer that the reader will rise above his fears and give prayerful consideration to the issues under discussion.

In the past year, I have frequently been comforted and reassured by Dave's fraternal support and by his insights as we both moved "through the tunnel." and I'm grateful that he has chosen to share this vital teaching with others.

Carn Catherwood
Big Sandy, Texas

Contents

Preface

Introduction
**The Worldwide Church of God as a
World Turned Upside Down** 21

Chapter One
The Demands of the Jewish Christians 31

Chapter Two
Biblically Defining the Law of Moses 37

Chapter Three
**How the Law of Moses was kept in Force
in the Worldwide Church of God** 45

Chapter Four
**Peter's Response to the Demands
of the Jewish Christians** 53

Chapter Five
**Peter's Vision:
Unclean Meats & Unclean Men** 61

Chapter Six
James' Counsel to the Gentiles 71

Chapter Seven
Eat Whatever Is Set Before You 77

Chapter Eight
**Are the Annual Festivals Part
of the Law of Moses?**   83

Chapter Nine
Categories of Proof   95

Chapter Ten
**The Verse Herbert Armstrong
Couldn't Explain**   109

Chapter Eleven
**Colossians 2:16-17
as the Bible Explains It**   119

Chapter Twelve
Common Sense About Galatians   135

Chapter Thirteen
Doubtful Disputations   145

Chapter Fourteen
But What About the Sabbath?   163

Chapter Fifteen
Pursuing the Character Ideal   179

Footnotes and References   191

Bibliography   195

Index   197

Preface

This book spins out of a time of crisis in the Worldwide Church of God, a church in which I have been a baptized member since 1960 and an ordained minister since 1963. As much or more than other Christian denominations, Worldwide Church of God members diligently tried to live by the various laws we found in the Bible, paying particular attention to the those given to ancient Israel in the Old Testament. As a result, members of the Worldwide Church of God did not eat "unclean meats" such as pork and shellfish, paid not one but two, sometimes three tithes, observed a seventh-day (Saturday) sabbath and celebrated annual festivals such as the Days of Unleavened Bread and the Feast of Tabernacles.

The 1990's have been a time of considerable doctrinal change and reform for us. One of the biggest lessons we have learned, rather belatedly, I admit, is that the law of Moses is not required for salvation. This came as a shock because, unlike members of most mainstream denominations, we in the Worldwide Church of God truly were Christians living under the law of Moses.

Thankfully, most of our members have come to understand and agree with these doctrinal changes even though that task has usually not been easy for them.

Others have condemned the changes as unscriptural deception and left to form new churches, seeking to maintain the doctrines and teachings established by the church's late founder and Pastor General, Herbert W. Armstrong. A sizeable number, which have come to be known as "the unaligned," are still angry, confused, or disillusioned, and no longer seem to be attending any church.

Such reactions to sweeping changes are sad but entirely predictable. Families have been divided—and that includes my own family. Friends and brethren now attend different churches. Sadly, some regard each other with a certain suspicion and distrust, if not downright hostility. A once united ministry of brothers in Christ is now split into three or four camps competing for the loyalties of a once united flock. This has been hard and very painful for everyone concerned, all the more so because we were once so close as members of one body sharing a common belief and practice.

Despite these difficulties, I sincerely believe that doctrinal changes in the Worldwide Church of God were necessary and I find them well supported by Scripture, but I've observed that many still don't understand those changes and are having emotional difficulty coping with them. I have also observed that some of our most vigorous opponents have very little grasp of the issues, and tend to revert to well-learned doctrinaire arguments from the past.

Disunity among Christians is not new. Discord erupted in the early New Testament Church between the Jewish and Gentile converts over the very same issues that have so recently divided the ministry and brethren in the Worldwide Church of God. Despite the painful contentions that afflicted the church, the first century apostles and elders labored mightily to "keep the unity of the Spirit in the bond of peace" (Eph. 4:4). Today, many of our ministers, myself included, are sorely grieved by the dissension and discord that has virtually torn our church asunder. God expects us to fulfill our calling as a "ministry of reconciliation" (II Cor. 5:18) and it is to that end that I have written this book. My own deeply held conviction is that there is, in fact, not all that much that divides us, and that what does could be overcome with patience, tolerance, and better understanding. I'd like nothing more than to see the breaches between families and friends healed and the harmony among our brethren restored.

Reflecting on my own experiences over the past thirty-five years, I've lived through many of the church's ups-and-downs, and have been acquainted with more than a few of its "movers and shakers." Since my first exposure to the <u>Plain Truth</u> as a teenager in 1958, I've been close to the sometimes turbulent issues and events that have shaped us as a church. As both a lay member and minister, I have had the privilege of seeing both the public and private face of the Worldwide Church of God.

I attended Ambassador College—now Ambassador University—from 1959 to 1963, and was ordained into the ministry after graduation on May 25, 1963. I pastored congregations in Texas, Ohio, and Kentucky before returning to Ambassador as an instructor in 1968.

At Ambassador I taught Speech and Bible classes, including the Epistles of Paul. I became thoroughly acquainted with Paul's writings, as we then understood them, as well as New Testament church history. As early as the 1970's I began to wrestle with what appeared to me to be doctrinal inconsistencies. It was difficult to explain certain scriptures, such as Galatians 3 ("the law that was added"), and I openly shared these problems with my students, allowing for possibilities other than those we traditionally taught.

While never part of the church hierarchy's inner circle, I knew and was influenced by many of the leading ministers and personalities in the church. These men were my teachers, preachers, mentors, and examples. They shaped my thinking, my understanding, my *life*.

So I know from long exposure and study the teachings and doctrines of the Worldwide Church of God. I also know the people, the personalities, the human side—the sometimes *very* human side—of this church.

I absorbed what my mentors had to give by way of example and instruction, but I never felt I was addicted to any man's personality, including that of the church's charismatic founder, Herbert W. Armstrong. I respect those who have taught me and gone before me in the faith, as we understood it, but I haven't been blind to their humanity any more than any of them, or any of you who may know me, have been blind to mine.

One of the most memorable days in my life was January 19th, 1986, the day of Herbert Armstrong's funeral in Pasadena, California. Everyone who had ever been anyone in the Worldwide Church of God was there, it seemed. The death of Mr. Armstrong was a pivotal event in the lives of most church members.

Right after the funeral service I stood only a few feet away from both the deceased Armstrong senior, now in his casket, and the living Armstrong junior, Garner Ted, now visibly in a state of grief and shock. I was deep in my own thoughts trying to sort out the meaning of the day's events, when Joseph W. Tkach, the man designated by Herbert Armstrong to be his successor, came over to me and announced, to my astonishment, that I was one of three men chosen to be the new presenters on the church's World Tomorrow telecast. The great irony of the occasion was, of course, that Garner Ted Armstrong, the man who, under different and better circumstances would have been the logical heir apparent and successor to his father, was standing almost within earshot.

It occurred to me on the way home, that this was the day that the Worldwide Church of God, Ambassador College, <u>The Plain Truth</u>, and the World Tomorrow telecast all ceased to be part of an Armstrong empire controlled by an Armstrong dynasty. Thereafter, you didn't have to be an Armstrong, or one of an inner circle of "leading men" to have a significant role in "The Work." Dave Albert was even going to do the World Tomorrow telecast! Now *that* took some getting used to for me, my wife, and for a good many others, no doubt.

But do the telecast I did, for the next seven years of my life, and those years, once again, put me in close touch with the inner workings of the church during the administration of Joseph Tkach, Sr. From time to time, I admit, he and I had some emphatic differences of opinion about the telecast. One of these got quite forcefully expressed at a weekly Tuesday morning "TRM" (Television Review Meeting) when I took both exception and some offense to a comment Mr. Tkach made. I took his criticism personally—he later explained he hadn't meant it that way—and unfortunately my reply was blunt and not at all tactful. Mr. Tkach bounded out of his executive chair looking to those present—myself included—as though he was planning to "lay hands on" Dave Albert! He had been a champion boxer in his Navy days and could be pretty feisty at times. But the argument, which of course never came to blows, quickly subsided, we both apologized, and after the meeting he put his arm around my shoulder and told me to treat the whole thing as though it never happened, something I was very glad to do. In hindsight, the incident was more comical and amusing than life threatening, but that fact wasn't altogether clear to everyone at the time!

I mean Mr. Tkach no disrespect in recounting this story. Far from it. He did only right by me, gave me not only a great deal of autonomy on the telecast but also his full support. I loved, admired, and respected the man, and found him easy to work for, very generous and kind. Those who worked closely with him and knew him well would say the same. When Joseph Tkach died in 1995, I counted it one of the greatest honors of my life to be asked to perform the eulogy at his memorial service at Ambassador University, here in Big Sandy, Texas.

I feel that Mr. Tkach was an unsung hero in the World-wide Church of God. It would not have been easy for *any-one* to have been Herbert Armstrong's successor. Mr. Armstrong was, after all, the founder of what was origi-nally the Radio Church of God and later became the World-wide Church of God. He pioneered The Plain Truth maga-zine and The World Tomorrow telecast back in the 1930's. He raised up Ambassador College on three campuses.

Herbert Armstrong was a man of vision with an unusually forceful, dynamic and sometimes rather dogmatic personality. I'll never forget the first time I saw him; it was 1959, and I was a freshman at Ambassador College. Soon after arriving on campus, I walked into the library and heard someone speaking energetically in the solarium. Even with his back to me, the man cast an aura that seemed to fill the entire first floor of the library. Though I had never seen him in person, there was no mistaking who it was. The shock of white hair, the booming voice, the emphatic gestures left no doubt that this was none other than Herbert W. Armstrong.

As the church's Pastor General, he was a hard act to follow. He was like a spiritual father figure to tens of thousands, and when he died the church received a blow from which it would never fully recover.

Joseph Tkach could never be the larger-than-life leader Herbert Armstrong had been, a fact that, to his credit, he knew from the beginning. To many he seemed like an interloper somehow unworthy or unqualified. Perhaps he was seen by others as an unloved step parent who could never be the church's "real daddy."

Mr. Tkach was thrust into a difficult role, but he conducted himself at all times with good grace and humor, including the ability to laugh at himself, one of his most endearing traits. He never took himself too seriously, as I suspect others would have, and he never let his office overwhelm him. A talented leader in his own right, he applied his strengths to uplift and edify the church of which he was now the head.

Later, when faced with momentous doctrinal decisions, he had the unsparing courage to follow Christ's lead in spite of the consequences. He knew the church was mired in legalism, shackled to an Old Covenant/law of Moses theology, and far too preoccupied with prophecy, and he determinedly set out to correct it.

Sadly, in some circles, Joseph Tkach is hated and despised as an apostate and heretic. I have before me a venomous letter from a former church member who concludes his tirade by insisting that "God struck him down for the changes he was making" because he "sold out to Satan's deception."

Joseph W. Tkach lived a full, active, and most useful life for nearly "three score and ten" years. Having lived till age 68, he probably had a longer life than either Peter or Paul. God took him, it's true. God will take us all in time. It is for those of us who remain, including his son, Joseph Tkach (Jr.), to follow where God leads, and that is what I hope we are all doing, to the best of our ability and understanding. Over the years, one scripture more than any other has guided and inspired my ministry—the one Paul quotes from the Psalms, "I *believed*, therefore have I spoken" (I Cor. 4:13).

I believed a lot of what I learned from Herbert Armstrong, and still do. The man had a way of inspiring people to study their Bibles. His understanding wasn't perfect; *nobody's* is. But he had many good things to impart to his followers, and I am not ashamed in the slightest to say I was one of them.

I've come to understand that the doctrinal legacy Herbert Armstrong gave to the Worldwide Church of God was not the *pure* truth nor the *whole* truth, nor at times, the *plain* truth. Mr. Armstrong was not infallible and never claimed to be. He often admitted in his later years that there were problems facing the church that his failing vision, hearing, and health simply did not permit him to address. He freely acknowledged that others after him would have to tackle these problems which, unfortunately, were building up in the church like flood waters behind a dam.

And that is exactly what happened. Pressure continued to mount all through Joseph W. Tkach's administration to examine pivotal issues emanating from the Old Covenant/New Covenant controversy, but he was rather limited in how much he could do or say, given the church's great emotional attachment to Herbert Armstrong and the precarious nature of his own leadership. Toward the end of his life the dam burst, and he was faced with the unpleasant decision whether to placate those who wanted to try to resurrect the "golden years" of the church and maintain the doctrinal status quo, or to call the church to repent of its errors and change, which he knew would wrench it out of its theological comfort zone. To his credit, Mr. Tkach chose to make the difficult but necessary doctrinal changes, thus setting a whole new course for the Worldwide Church of God.

The search for truth is active and ongoing, not static or fixed in a certain time or place. The Armstrong years were not "the golden age" of Biblical wisdom and truth, nor were the Tkach years. Truth isn't found in a nostalgic bygone era, like some kind of Camelot kingdom that tragically slipped away. But that's how some see it, I'm afraid.

Sadly, some remain mired and anchored in the past. They yearn for the spiritual "good old days," forgetting God's admonition, "Do not say, 'Why were the former days better than these?' For you do not inquire wisely concerning this" (Eccles. 7:10).

Let us then choose the way of the wise. The task before us today is to learn and live the truth and to share it with others. We must go forward. Yet, many are still dazed and confused and attrition of our membership continues. Because these people are my brethren, my family, my friends and fellow ministers, I want to do everything in my power to help, to "establish, strengthen, and settle" those who are currently troubled. That is why I have written this book. It is my personal message, in my own voice, straight from the heart.

Thank you in advance for giving it your careful and prayerful consideration.

David Albert
Big Sandy, Texas
February, 1996

The Worldwide Church of God as a World Turned Upside Down

Every once in a great while a change occurs that is so sweeping, so total, that it can only be described as "revolutionary." It is the kind of change that seems to turn the world upside down. Such revolutionary change can happen in the world of science, religion or politics, and when it does, much turmoil and confusion are the inevitable results. New facts and information come to light which cannot be readily explained, posing a serious challenge to the old way of thinking. This provokes an unexpected crisis which then triggers an even less anticipated, often unwelcome solution, after which the world is never the same again.

One of the best examples of such a change occurred during the Middle Ages when science shifted from an earth-centered to a sun-centered world view. Prior to the fourth century A.D. the earth was believed to be fixed and immovable, the exact center of the universe. As anyone could plainly see, the sun, moon, planets and stars all went around the earth, a phenomenon that even the Bible seemed to corroborate, for wasn't the sun "like a bridegroom coming out of his chamber...rising from one end of heaven, and *its circuit to the other end*"(Psalm 19:5)? To declare otherwise branded one a fool and a heretic.

But one observant astronomer named Copernicus said that certain phenomena *he* could plainly see, such as the phases of the moon, suggested a sun-centered universe. Some time later a simple, low-powered telescope in the hands of Galileo revealed that there were also moon-like phases of Venus and moons of Jupiter. These discoveries conclusively proved Copernicus had been right even though he was forced by the Pope and the Church to recant his "heretical" views. But when the Copernican view of astronomy and the known universe was finally embraced, the world was forever changed. It was, to use a term from math and science, a "paradigm shift" of vast and sweeping proportions.

The now-popular term "paradigm shift" was coined in 1962 by scientific historian Thomas Kuhn. In his compelling book, <u>The Structure of Scientific Revolutions</u> he describes the nature of radical, revolutionary change, and the stressful, powerful consequences that accompany such change. Yes, the same kind of change that we in the Worldwide Church of God experienced when the world—our world—was turned upside down.

Jesus Christ and his disciples had this same unsettling effect on the religious world of their day. Notice the accusation leveled against Paul and Silas after they preached the Gospel in the Jewish synagogue at Thessalonica. An angry mob dragged one of the disciples before the magistrate crying, "These men who have turned the world upside down have come here too" (Acts 17:5-6).

As did the devout Jews of the first century, we also found our neat, orderly theology turned upside down by a radical paradigm shift. We've no doubt observed in our brethren, our friends—ourselves!—the gamut of responses, from eager, grateful acceptance to massive, close-minded resistance. Like many of you, I know all too well about and crisis and change, turmoil and confusion, doubt, panic and fear.

In times of turmoil and sweeping change, good people *on both sides of the conflict* do rash, foolish, and sometimes even sinful things that hurt and offend others. Ideally, it shouldn't happen, especially among people calling themselves Christians, but sadly, it does. We all have stories to tell—amusing, disturbing, perhaps even horrifying—yet these ought not compromise our objective search for the truth. Tales about who did what to whom, and how awful it was, etc., often provoke an emotional response that seems somehow convincing, but this also can distract us from the key issues. I have discovered that truth is not determined by personal incidents, anecdotes or "war stories," no matter how compelling. *For Christians truth is determined by the Word of God*, and I have tried, not always successfully, I admit, to focus on God's Word, not personal feelings.

Thomas Kuhn makes two especially valuable points that for me, provide a helpful framework for understanding the trauma of change we have experienced of late in the church.

First, as the earth-centered/sun-centered debate so clearly demonstrates, one set of facts can be interpreted two different ways! Everyone in that historic, scientific-theological debate was looking at the *same* earth, *same* sun and moon, *same* stars and planets, but each opposing faction understood and explained what they saw in two *very* different ways. As Kuhn observed, "Philosophers of science have repeatedly demonstrated that more then one theoretical construction can always be placed on a given collection of data." In the religious world, we can look at the same Bible, read and quote the same familiar verses, and interpret them two—or more!—radically different ways.

Paul's statements on the law are a classic Biblical example. Some who read his epistles are convinced Paul is against law and does away with it. Others read the same letters and find much support in them for keeping the law. Same evidence, two different interpretations.

But let me share something startling I learned from Kuhn about those two opposing views of the universe: *they both worked*! It wasn't as though people under the earth-centered Ptolemaic system couldn't predict the appearance of the stars and planets, have and use an accurate calendar, or plant and harvest their crops in the right seasons. No, in fact, in many ways *the old system worked every bit as well as the new*, and as Kuhn points out, "...for the stars, Ptolemaic astronomy *is still widely used today* as an engineering approximation." There were only a few areas where the old system proved unsatisfactory, in the prediction of equinoxes, for example. Overall, however, it provided an *adequate and workable* explanation of the universe. The old earth-centered paradigm was "pretty good," but for precise and exacting men of science "pretty good" is not good enough—which brings me to point two.

While it's true that two competing theories can offer reasonable interpretations of the same set of facts (or scriptures, as we'll see), *one*, if it's true, will fit the facts *better*. A flawed theory, no matter how useful it has been in the past, will sooner or later experience what the scientific community calls a "breakdown" leading to a crisis. Thus, Kuhn advises, "It makes a great deal of sense to ask which of the two actual and competing theories fits the facts *better*."

I found that bit of advice especially helpful and enlightening because I had a religious world view for thirty-five years of my life that *seemed to work remarkably well*. You have all heard the saying, "If it ain't broke, don't fix it." Well, I didn't think our theological paradigm was seriously "broke" and I didn't see many places where it needed to be fixed. That's why initially I deeply resented the attempts of those who wanted to fix what wasn't "broke"!

Along with nearly 100,000 others in the Worldwide Church of God, I believed that we alone were *the* people of God—the one and only true church preaching the one true gospel, a notion I enthusiastically taught and preached for years. We had a way of life that seemed to work well, in addition to certain distinctive features that set us apart from "the world"—including most of the *Christian* world. These we called "identifying signs" of the true church, which included observing the seventh-day sabbath and annual holy days. We didn't eat pork or other "unclean meats," we paid our tithes, and some of us honestly believed that anyone who didn't do all of these things was headed for the Great Tribulation, or maybe worse.

Our gospel emanated *from a church* but was aimed primarily *at certain nations* such as the United States, Britain, and most of western Europe, whom we believed to be descendants of the "lost ten tribes" of ancient Israel. We sincerely felt that a major part of the church's "Great Commission" included warning these modern Israelitish nations of their sins before they were sent into national captivity, as was ancient Israel. We had plenty of Scriptures to support our viewpoint, almost all of them, you may be sure, from the Old Testament. Ironically, we enthusiastically devoted ourselves to this task but with the foregone conclusion that these nations *would not* repent! They would, however, have received "a warning and a witness," and thus we would have fulfilled our commission. You'll still find this heavy, nationalistic theme of warning the modern Israelites in the publications of the various Worldwide Church of God splinter groups. The notion that the gospel should be preached on a national basis is central to their world view.

I, like many of you reading this, gave my time, life, and resources to a church whose belief system, for the most part, worked well, and seemed to fit the facts of the Bible. We had a Biblical paradigm that answered all of our questions, generally to our satisfaction. We also had certain ways of handling issues that didn't adapt to our theological views. We even had a name for Bible verses that did not fit our religious paradigm—we called them "difficult scriptures." *Everyone* in or formerly in the Worldwide Church of God has to be *very* familiar with that phrase!

I was even more familiar with "difficult scriptures" than most. Not only did I grapple with them as an Ambassador College student, but as a speech and homiletics instructor I must have assigned and evaluated hundreds of what we called "difficult scripture sermonettes." In hindsight, I believe these mandatory assignments were placed in the curriculum not only for speech training, but also as a means of indoctrinating students with our theology in areas that would otherwise undermine our theological paradigm.

So fledgling speakers and potential ministers were, for example, expected to explain our Old Covenant-based teaching regarding "clean and unclean meats" in the light of New Testament verses such as Romans 14:14, "I know and am convinced by the Lord Jesus that *there is nothing unclean of itself*; but to him who considers anything to be unclean, to him it is unclean."

I Timothy 4:4 was another verse that required tangled logic to explain away, "For *every* creature of God is *good*"—for *food* as we see in verse 3—"and *nothing is to be refused* if it is received with thanksgiving." I look back now, amazed, and ask myself just which part of that "difficult scripture" was difficult? Was it the "every"? Or the "good"? Or the "nothing to be refused"? No, obviously there is nothing really difficult about these verses *unless you've got a bias or a prejudice against what they plainly say*! Or unless you're stuck in a paradigm that cannot adequately explain the facts.

We had all kinds of clever and convoluted ways that we carefully learned and rehearsed in order to handle these *many* difficult—to *us*!—scriptures. Unfortunately, these passages didn't fit our Biblical paradigm any better than the phases of the moons of Jupiter fit Ptolemy's earth-centered astronomy. We *made* them conform to our doctrinal perspective. But we always said it was the *other* people who were guilty of "twisting the scriptures" (II Pet. 3:16)!

Well, the internal crisis that was brewing came to a head in 1994-1995. It was as though someone had discovered the telescope and was calling our attention to issues that no longer could be explained adequately or accurately by our existing paradigm, "clean and unclean meats" being one of the better examples. The generic label that best encompassed these new-to-us discoveries was the "New Covenant." Facts about the New Covenant that were in our Bibles all along were coming to light because of the courageous and often unpopular leadership of Joseph W. Tkach. At this point, we were rapidly moving toward the breakdown and crisis point in the model described by Kuhn.

History demonstrates that progress in science is not linear; that is, it is not a steady, uninterrupted process. Rather, science advances along a plateau executing what Kuhn calls "normal science," nicely solving its puzzles and problems based on its known laws, theories, and paradigms—until something comes along that "upsets the apple cart", and the system starts to break down. This is called a "counterinstance," a phenomenon or discovery that seems to defy the known "law"—in other words, a notable exception or an anomaly. What happens next, interestingly, parallels the current crisis in the Worldwide Church of God.

When new facts no longer fit the old theories, science shifts its attention from the "normal" to the "abnormal." More and more scientists learn of the new, solution-resistant problem. They attempt to "magnify the breakdown," by exploring all the ways in which the new data does not fit or operate within the previous framework of information.

> The anomaly itself now comes to be more generally recognized as such by the profession. More and more attention is devoted to it by more and more of the field's most eminent men. If it still continues to resist...many of them may come to view its resolution as *the* subject matter of their discipline. For the field will no longer look quite the same as it had earlier. [4]

I believe we as a church are at this very point right now in our history. For some time now, our best scholars have been exploring in-depth what Joseph W. Tkach sketched out for us in sermons and articles—the "plain truth," if you will, of the New Covenant. Kuhn explains that even in the world of science this willingness to accept and take up the challenge of the new takes faith—"faith that the new paradigm will succeed with the many large problems that confront it, knowing that the older paradigm has failed with a few." He adds, "Something must make at least a few scientists feel that the new proposal is on the right track." [5]

I saw many, including myself, take that leap of faith in spite of the obstacles. One by one a few brave ministers and members stood up and said, "Yes, I think this makes sense and we're on the right track." Others, as one might expect, thought those who did so had lost their minds, if not their souls.

But to counteract the first strong wave of opposition, another interesting phenomenon occurs. Kuhn explains, "But if a paradigm is ever to succeed it must gain some first supporters, men who will develop it to the point where *hard-headed arguments can be produced and multiplied*" (emphasis mine throughout).[6] Currently, some good "hard-headed" and strong Biblically-based arguments are coming to the fore in support of our new understanding. It is not easy work, to be sure, but I believe solid Biblical research will prevail in spite of the opposition.

Speaking of this first group of courageous supporters, Kuhn writes, "If they are competent, they will improve it, explore its possibilities, and show what it would be like to belong to the community guided by it. And as that goes on, if the paradigm is one destined to win its fight, the number and strength of the persuasive arguments in its favor will increase."[7]

Currently, Worldwide Church of God scholars are working to deepen and improve our new doctrinal understanding and to explore its possibilities. Following their example, I will, in the chapters that follow, carefully and critically examine the evidence—the *Biblical* evidence—that fell outside our former doctrinal/theological paradigm. I will begin in Acts 15 and focus on the law of Moses.

The Worldwide Church of God, following the teachings of Herbert Armstrong, unwittingly bound itself to the law of Moses despite clear Bible teaching to the contrary.

As the most striking illustration of this, I will discuss the church's doctrine on "clean and unclean meats" for here we have the most glaring example of a "counterinstance," an Old Covenant requirement made binding on New Testament Christians.

For both current and former members of the Worldwide Church of God, the moons of Jupiter can be found by focusing one's observations on Acts 15 and that very first Jerusalem Conference. Let us now turn our attention to that pivotal conference, which was responsible for turning the early church—and now the Worldwide Church of God—literally upside down.

Chapter One

The Demands
of the
Jewish Christians

I come now to the centerpiece of my case against certain ideas that were at the core of what I believed, taught, and practiced for thirty-five years in the Worldwide Church of God. It is a strange thing—to repudiate publicly much of what one formerly held sacred. But the choice before me is clear— to continue in what I now see as error or to bring my beliefs and practices squarely in line with God's Word. Put that way, the choice is easy. I must go with what is clearly revealed in the Word.

It is important for every Christian to understand the pivotal importance of Acts 15. The issues before the early church on that historic occasion were these: What are the terms and conditions of membership for new believers? And what is *required* for salvation?

The "new believers" referred to in Acts 15 were *Gentile* converts, but the decision of that first church council applies to *all* believers, then and now. Acts 15 explains what is required and expected of all new converts and, just as critically, *what is not.*

This is important to me because when I came to Christ and into Christian fellowship with the Worldwide Church of God, prerequisites other than those found in Acts 15 were required of me. Worse yet, after my ordination into the ministry

31

in 1963 I required of new believers the same terms and conditions that were required of me. Terms and conditions, I have discovered, God himself rescinded nearly two thousand years ago.

I have baptized approximately a thousand people in the course of my ministry and counseled for baptism many more. I now recognize that I withheld from baptism some who doubtless had faith in Christ but did not at that time meet the requirements of the church. Sad to say, in times past we bound and required things on earth that were not bound in heaven. This compels me to acknowledge publicly where I—where we as the ministry and leadership of the church—went wrong. Not *intentionally* wrong. We were sincere and well meaning, but we were wrong nonetheless, and it's time to say so and to stand corrected by our Lord and Master Jesus Christ.

Although we missed the obvious in Acts 15, Christian scholars all along have known precisely what was at stake at the Jerusalem Conference of Acts 15. One commentator writes,

> Outstanding in the history of the apostolic church is this apostolic convention at Jerusalem and the spirit and manner in which it settled the great question regarding what was necessary for salvation and thus for membership in the Christian Church.

My own experience illustrates that despite how basic this subject may be, and how apparent the answer is to some, *hundreds of thousands of Christians* from what I'll call the "legalistic tradition" are still confused about the terms and conditions for salvation and membership in the Church of God and Body of Christ. The term "legalistic" may be offensive to some, I realize, but the great debate in Acts 15 began with a group of Christians who argued that believers had to keep certain *laws* in order to be saved and to partake of Christian fellowship. There is no escaping that these demands were legalistic, and neither can we escape the fact that in modern times some, myself included, have made the *very same kinds of demands of new believers*. If you are struggling with these issues, and I know many of you are, please try to keep an open mind and hear the Word of God on this critical subject. Remember the good example of the Bereans, "These were more fair-minded than those in Thessalonica, in that they received the word with all readiness, *and searched the Scriptures daily to find out whether these things were so*" (Acts 17:11).

Let's look now at the *two-fold* nature of the demands made by the legalistic contingent at the Jerusalem Conference, "And certain men came down from Judea and taught the brethren, 'unless you are circumcised according to the custom of Moses, you cannot be saved'" (Acts 15:1).

One demand was *circumcision*, the covenant sign God made with Abraham and Israel. Note that circumcision is not viewed as an optional recommendation, but a requirement *essential for salvation*. "Without circumcision," they were saying, "you cannot be saved."

Now if that were the only issue of Acts 15, I wouldn't be writing this book, and for me and thousands of others in the legalistic tradition there simply would be *no problem*. Why not? Because *everybody* knows that circumcision isn't required for salvation and no Christian church I know of, including the Worldwide Church of God, has ever required it.

But circumcision is only one of *two* demands found in Acts 15. The other is found in verse 5, "But some of the sect of the Pharisees who believed rose up, saying, 'It is necessary to circumcise them, *and to command them to keep the law of Moses*.'"

So it wasn't only circumcision, but circumcision *and the law of Moses* that some believed were necessary conditions for salvation.

It is important to note that these demands are coming from believing Jewish *Christians*. These were people who had already believed on and accepted Christ as their Savior; they were not unconverted Jewish opponents of the Gospel as Lenski clearly explains,

> Some have a wrong conception of them, as though they rejected the entire gospel, the entire Christ, and preached only salvation by law. But they were believers in Christ and the gospel, members of the church at Jerusalem, but they erred in a most dangerous point, namely in wanting to append to the gospel and Christ the requirement of circumcision (that most especially) and of other Mosaic regulations. *They thought the gospel incomplete without this addition.* [2]

So these are *Christians* who believed one must obey certain laws in order to be saved, *Christians* who thought notable features of the Old Covenant God made through Moses must be continued under the New Covenant of Jesus Christ. Perhaps it should come as no surprise that there are still Christians today who think that certain key features of the Law of Moses need to be appended to the Christian gospel. I should know! I was one of them for thirty-five years.

Make no mistake, circumcision is inexorably linked to the law of Moses—they are not separate issues. Notice what Paul said, "I, Paul, say to you that if you become circumcised, Christ will profit you nothing. And I testify again to every man who becomes circumcised that he is a debtor *to keep the whole law*" (Gal. 5:3-4). Strangely, we in the Worldwide Church of God thought these two requirements could be separated. We rejected circumcision, but somehow kept the law of Moses, minus the sacrifices and certain ceremonies.

Circumcision was for the Jews what baptism is for Christians today—the formal entry rite or ceremony into a whole way of life and a declaration of one's willingness to adhere to that way of life. Just as we are baptized into Christ and Christianity, Jewish proselytes were circumcised into the law of Moses and Judaism.

Kistemaker, in his New Testament Commentary, writes of the believing Pharisees,

> They determine that all Christians, whether Jew or Gentile, are obligated to obey the entire law of Moses, and that includes circumcision.... The Christianity of these Pharisees is overshadowed by their emphasis on the Mosaic law. They assert that the development of the church can take place only when believers adhere to all the stipulations of the Old Testament. *They virtually demand that every Gentile become a Jew before he can be a Christian.* [3]

At first it seems as though many Jews thought Jesus only brought a "higher" form of Judaism. They assumed that Christ, being a Jew, laid the foundation of Christianity on a Jewish base. This was a most understandable error. Until that time, nothing had been said or done to suggest that circumcision and the law of Moses had been nullified. It appeared that the old paradigm was still very much in place.

Kistemaker summarizes Acts 15:1-5, "These Jewish Christians contended that every convert must first be circumcised and then be taught to observe the law of Moses." [4]

Lenski, also speaking of the Jewish Christians writes,

> Their teaching is quoted in brief. Circumcision is necessary for salvation....if circumcision was essential...then what about all else that Moses had required? Consistency would have soon introduced *the entire legal system.* [5]

Just as Paul stated in Galatians 5, circumcision logically leads to the observance of "the whole law." It's a package deal.

Lenski, however, appreciates how difficult it was for the Jewish Christians to change,

> Thus it came about that, when the new covenant was established, circumcision together with the entire old covenant was at an end. Circumcision, the whole old Mosaic system, had lost its import and efficacy. *It was hard for Jews who had grown*[6] *up in this system to realize this truth.*

And it is hard still for those of us who have been ensnared by legalism to grasp this truth, even though these issues were settled nearly 2,000 years ago.

James Dunn, commenting on Galatians 5, makes the same inevitable connection between circumcision and the whole law: "To accept circumcision...would be to revert to slavery (5:1). *It would involve adopting the whole Jewish way of life*, that is[7] reverting to the old epoch of life under the law (5:3)."

What the Jewish Christians demanded is clear—circumcision *and* the law of Moses. Let's now understand how the Bible uses and defines the term "law of Moses."

Chapter Two

Biblically Defining
the Law of Moses

In Acts 15 we find the loose string, which if pulled, unravels the whole garment of legalism. The terms and conditions for new believers is clearly set, and the debate over whether Christians must keep the law of Moses in order to be saved is settled once and for all.

Looking back, it seems strange that as a minister and teacher who thought he knew his Bible I—we—never understood this pivotal chapter. It isn't as though we in the Worldwide Church of God ignored Acts 15 or avoided discussing the Jerusalem Council. We often used this passage to explain church government and to show how doctrinal issues should be settled in the church. We also understood that this first apostolic council decided that circumcision was not required of the Gentiles.

We knew the command, "unless you are circumcised according to the custom taught by Moses, you cannot be saved," was abolished under the New Covenant, and neither Herbert Armstrong nor any minister of the Worldwide Church of God ever required that of a new convert.

What we failed to understand was that circumcision and obedience to the law of Moses go hand-in-hand. Obedience to one *means* obedience to the other. It is as though we never carefully read Acts 15:5, "The Gentiles must be circumcised *and* required to obey the law of Moses."

Obedience was not an either-or proposition. It was circumcision *and* the law of Moses, not circumcision *or* the law of Moses. As the Seventh-day Adventist Bible Commentary points out, "Circumcision was not the only requirement the Judaizers proposed to make of Christians. *It was only their entering wedge.*"[1]

In the Worldwide Church of God prior to 1995, we rarely discussed the term "law of Moses" in relation to our theology or world view. We would never have admitted that any of our doctrines or practices were based on "the law of Moses." Rather, we used the term "Law of God," or simply "God's Law," which meant almost everything we found required in the Bible—the commandments, statutes, judgments, and ordinances.

The principal exceptions to this were the animal sacrifices, which we knew were replaced by Christ's sacrifice, and circumcision, as already mentioned. Most everything else, we, at one time or another, tried to keep in some form, including the laws prohibiting mixed fabrics and even the agricultural land sabbaths. Much was written and preached about the Law of God, little, if anything, about the law of Moses.

The reason for this curious omission is now, I see in retrospect, rather obvious: We simply could not examine the implications of a law or legal code found in the Bible that was not required of Christians. To do so would have led to the wholesale destruction of our legalistic paradigm. We did not and could not associate a law with a mere man, Moses, and call it by his name. That would make the law seem, somehow, "humanly" devised, and therefore less spiritual, less authoritative, less binding. So we appropriated other adjectives to describe the law, such as, "spiritual," " eternal," and "immutable from Creation." Most, it seems, came to think of the law in absolute and universal terms.

We had no place in our paradigm for a law that was associated with a man, a time, a place, and a nation, or a law that was temporary or that could possibly be rescinded. The "Law of *God*" fit our paradigm, the "law of *Moses*" did not. Thus we couldn't see in Acts 15 what we didn't want to see, namely, **that within nearly two decades after the founding of the New Testament church, God inspired the apostles at the Jerusalem Council to declare that obedience to the law of Moses was NOT required for new believers and thus was NOT a requirement for salvation, church membership or fellowship.**

Bible Definitions of the Law of Moses

But just what *is* "the law of Moses?" My own understanding of the term as shaped by the Worldwide Church of God—and I'm sure it was the same for most of our members and ministers—was that it was principally the sacrifices and offerings, circumcision, and those things that were clearly ceremonial, such as wearing fringes on one's garments. Based on this teaching, I would have rejected utterly the idea that the law of Moses included the Sabbath and Holy Days, the land sabbaths, tithing—first, second, and third tithes!—and clean and unclean meats, what many call the kosher food laws. Some of these things, I realize, were relaxed somewhat over the years. But in the 1950's and '60's, we were taught that all true Christians were obligated to obey the "Law of God," and as ministers we diligently taught the law and even required potential members to begin obeying it before they could be baptized into the church.

39

To understand exactly the parameters of "the law of Moses"— as well as the issues involved in the Jerusalem Council debate—we need to properly define the term according to its Biblical and historical usage, not according to a theological paradigm created nearly 2,000 years later.

How is the term used in the Scriptures? Did Jesus use it, and if so, how? In Acts 15, what were new converts loosed *from*, and what, if anything, were they bound *to*? Were they loosed from sacrifices and circumcision, but bound to sabbaths, tithing, and kosher food laws? Just what *is* the law of Moses, according to the Bible?

It actually is quite easy to find answers in the Bible to these questions. Thankfully, you don't need to be a seminary-trained theologian with a graduate degree in biblical studies. With a Bible, an exhaustive concordance, an hour or two to devote to the study, and an open mind, you can discover "the plain truth," if you will, about the law of Moses.

There are approximately thirty verses or passages in the Bible linking the "law" with "Moses" as in "the law of Moses," "Moses' law," "Moses gave you the law," "the law came through Moses," etc. My own study located nineteen references in the Old Testament and eleven in the New— quite enough to provide a thorough and accurate picture of how the Bible uses the term "the law of Moses" and its variations.

Let me summarize these briefly for you and at the same time suggest that you study them later in greater detail. Let's highlight the Old Testament verses first.

You'll find the term "law of Moses" introduced and used at least four times in Deuteronomy; it describes the comprehensive legal code God gave to Israel (Deut. 1:5, 4:8, 31:9, 33:4). It also is linked specifically to Sinai, "The Lord came from Sinai and dawned over them from

Seir...from His right hand came a fiery law for them...'Moses commanded a law for us, a heritage of the congregation of Jacob'" (Deut. 33:2-4 NKJV).

Notice how the law of Moses is used in Joshua, especially Josh. 8:31-32. "A copy of the law of Moses" was written on large stones when Israel entered the promised land. The people reviewed the blessings they would receive for keeping it and the cursings they would suffer for breaking it. Nothing there suggests the law of Moses is only "sacrificial and ceremonial." Or worse yet, as one "under-the-law" minister tried to explain recently, "sacerdotal," or pertaining only to the priesthood! Joshua had Israel reiterate the *whole* law of Moses.

I Kings 2:3 gives us one of the best indications of the comprehensive nature of the law. "And keep the charge of the Lord your God: to walk in His ways, to keep His statutes, His commandments, His judgments, and His testimonies, *as it is written in the Law of Moses*...." How clear that the law of Moses includes the commandments, statutes and judgments, and not just sacrifices, ceremonies, and circumcision.

In II Chronicles we find the law of Moses used to prescribe burnt offerings and to describe Levitical duties (II Chron. 23:18; 30:16). Those, too, are *part* of the law of Moses.

The prophet Ezra preached the law of Moses to Judah after the Babylonian Captivity, which prompted Judah once again to keep the Feast of Tabernacles (Neh. 8). This indicates that the *authority for the annual festivals derives from what the Scriptures calls the law of Moses.*

The final Old Testament reference links the law of Moses to Sinai and to the statutes and judgments; there is no mention of sacrifices or circumcision (Mal. 4:4).

Even a brief tour of these Old Testament references acquaints us with the fact that the law of Moses is used in a comprehensive way to describe or refer to *the whole legal package God gave through Moses.* Because the Bible does not contradict itself, we should expect the New Testament to parallel this view. And as we shall see, it does.

How the New Testament Defines the Law of Moses

As we examine the New Testament references to the law of Moses, let's keep in mind why a proper definition of this term is so important. If the sabbath, holy days, food laws, and tithing were never a part of this narrowly defined sacrificial/ceremonial code called the law of Moses, then perhaps, it could be argued, they are binding on Christians after all. They are certainly described as "laws" in the Scripture, and if they are not part of the law of Moses, which was clearly done away, then they still must be in force! This was the doctrinal position maintained by the Worldwide Church of God prior to 1995.

However, if it can be proven that the law of Moses is broad, general and inclusive, and refers to *all* of the laws given to the children of Israel through Moses, then we must reconcile how individual laws subsumed in that larger body of law—which we all agree has been revoked—could be pulled out and arbitrarily declared "binding."

As we have seen, the law of Moses *is* used in the broadest possible sense in the Old Testament, and this pattern changes not at all in the New Testament.

In Luke 2:22, we are told Christ underwent the rites of "purification according to the Law of Moses." That is, he was circumcised and also consecrated, being a first-born Jewish male. Such rites are clearly ceremonial and are always accepted as part of the law of Moses.

By comparison, Jesus' use of the term "law of Moses" in Luke 24:44 could hardly be more sweeping. There, after his resurrection, he expounds to the disciples all the things that were written of him "in the Law of Moses, the Prophets, and the Psalms." This phrase has always been understood to mean the three-fold division of the Old Testament. The Law of Moses refers to the Pentateuch or first five books of the Bible, all of which Moses had a hand in writing, editing and/or preserving.

John uses the term prophetically when Philip announced to Nathaniel, "We have found the one Moses wrote about in the law" (John 1:45). In John 7:21-23 Jesus himself uses the term, referring to circumcision as a requirement of the Mosaic law. And in John 8:5, the scribes and Pharisees call on the law of Moses to justify their intention to stone the woman taken in adultery.

Paul states, "It is written in the law of Moses: 'Do not muzzle an ox while it is treading out the grain'" (I Cor. 9:9). Is this referring to a sacrifice or ceremony? No, it's a law given by God through Moses concerning the proper care of one's animals from which Paul draws a spiritual analogy about caring for the laborers in God's harvest.

The final New Testament reference is in Hebrews 10:28, which refers to those who rejected the law of Moses and died without mercy for their violations thereof.

Reflecting on the ways in which these New Testament passages define the law of Moses, it is untenable to insist that it refers merely to sacrificial and ceremonial laws.

Nowhere in God's Word is it limited to that meaning. Nor is it the sacrificial/ceremonial system that the Jewish Christians were trying to enjoin upon the Gentiles in Acts 15. These believing Jews, who had accepted Jesus as the Christ, were not demanding animal sacrifices of the Antiochan Gentile converts! The key issue presented in Acts, which we shall examine in some detail, focused specifically on food and dietary requirements, what Worldwide Church of God members have always called "clean and unclean meats."

As we have seen from this brief overview, the law of Moses includes commandments, statutes, judgments, offerings, priestly instructions, purification rites and laws concerning animal husbandry. It was *an entire legal package*, a comprehensive code, and the basis of the covenant God made with Israel at Sinai (Ex. 34:27). That is what all the Bible authors and persons quoted in the Bible, including Jesus Christ himself, meant when they used the term. Given the abundance of Bible definitions, there's really no need for confusion on this point, but let me now show how Herbert Armstrong managed to obscure the clear meaning of these verses, thereby keeping a key feature of the law of Moses in place.

Chapter Three

How the Law of Moses was kept in Force in the Worldwide Church of God

In February, 1958, The Plain Truth ran an article written by Herbert Armstrong entitled "Is *All* Animal Flesh *Good for Food?*" which carried the subtitle "Here is a straight-forward Bible answer, giving New Testament teaching."

According to the Worldwide Church of God literature index, this article had a long publishing history and was probably read by millions of Plain Truth readers. It was rerun in The Plain Truth in 1973, 1978, and 1983. It was then incorporated into a booklet entitled Personal Health which was published in 1983, 1985, and as late as 1988—two years after Herbert Armstrong's death. For decades, it defined church doctrine on the subject.

In the original 1958 article, after bold sub-section titles such as, "You are Eating POISON!" "What the Great Architect of Your Stomach Instructs," Herbert Armstrong attempts to establish the authority of the food laws.

Speaking of God's regulation of man's diet, he writes, "When the first revelation of God came to man through Moses God instructed man as to which kinds of animal flesh man ought or ought not to eat. You will find this list in Leviticus 11 and Deuteronomy 14." [1]

45

So far so good. We have God, Moses, and the food laws in their proper location in the Bible. He is, at that point, so close! It would be but one short step to the truth of the matter—that the dietary laws were part of the law of Moses—but that's a step he never takes. Instead, we're introduced to a new kind of law never mentioned in the Bible that neatly sidesteps the problems associated with the law of Moses and Acts 15. What "law" is this?

> This is *basic law*—a revelation from God to man about which kinds of foods will properly digest and assimilate in the human system, and which will not. It is not a part of God's great SPIRITUAL LAW, summed up in the Ten Commandments. Neither is it part of the ceremonial, ritualistic, or sacrificial laws later abolished at the crucifixion of Christ (emphasis his). [2]

These "basic laws" he subsequently calls "physical laws," a term never used in the Bible. Breaking them, according to Mr. Armstrong, results in something else the Bible nowhere speaks of, and that is "physical sin." He writes, "We must realize, there are physical laws working in our bodies, regulating our health. *This meat question has to do with these laws*." [3]

According *to whom*? This statement was made without Biblical evidence or proof of any kind. But notice how neatly it solves the problem. Suddenly there is a new category of laws, neither spiritual nor ceremonial, neither God's law nor Moses' law, and for which there is no Biblical basis for discussion. We're introduced to a whole new area of "law" for which no Scriptures apply and for which Herbert Armstrong has become the sole and final authority.

Under the subhead, "Not Ceremonial Law," the possibility that the dietary laws may be part of the law of Moses is completely dismissed. "The instruction in Leviticus 11 and Deuteronomy 14, then, is not some ritualistic regulation for the Mosaic period only."[4] Why not? Because they are "basic laws," and "physical laws" which regulate our bodies and promote good health.

Many still try to defend the food laws in terms of their alleged health benefits, but it is important to recognize that nowhere at any time in God's Word do we find foods clean or unclean discussed, prohibited or approved based on their nutritional value or their effects on the human body. God never indicated that he gave these laws to Israel so they could be the healthiest nation, the one with the best digestion or the cleanest digestive tracts. But that's where Mr. Armstrong centers his argument— on the health benefits of keeping the dietary laws.

Let me develop that point a little further since some still seem quite confused about it. The food laws found in their fullest form in Leviticus 11 are part of a whole set of laws that could best described as ceremonial laws. They could also be described as the "holiness laws." When God explains his reasons for instituting them, he does not appeal to health but to holiness, "For I am the Lord your God. You shall therefore sanctify yourself, and you shall be holy; for I am holy" (Lev. 11:44).

We find the same rationale applied to things clean and the unclean in the other "food chapter," Deuteronomy 14, "You are a holy people to the Lord Your God, and the Lord has chosen you to be a people for himself, a special treasure above all peoples who are on the face of the earth" (Deut. 14:2).

These are the laws that gave the nation of Israel its preferred status, separated them from other nations and made them special. These laws pronounced many things "unclean" or defiled beside food. Menstruating women were unclean, as were women who had just given birth. Dead animals were unclean. Men who had an issue of semen in the night were unclean. Anyone who touched anything or anyone that was unclean was unclean, etc. These are the laws of ceremonial or ritual defilement. Take time to study them in the Book of Leviticus. Most have no problem understanding their ceremonial nature and wouldn't think of requiring them today. While many of them may have certain health benefits, their true purpose is best summed up in Leviticus 20:2-26,

> "You shall distinguish between clean beasts and unclean, between unclean birds and clean, and you shall not make yourselves abominable by any beast or by bird...which I have separated from you as unclean. And you shall be holy to Me, for I the Lord am holy, and *have separated you from the peoples*, that you should be mine."

God declares that the purpose of these laws is to make the nation of Israel separate and distinct—and they most definitely had that effect. They were appropriate to his work on a national basis with a chosen and separate people. But under the New Covenant, when the plan of God became universal, a plan for *all* peoples, not just a chosen people, these laws become a barrier and a stumbling block that had to be removed.

I hope that adds to your understanding of the purpose for these laws and demonstrates why defending them for their physical health benefits is a deeply flawed argument and virtually irrelevant from a Biblical perspective. When Mr. Armstrong introduces the notions of poison, health, and digestion into this Biblical discussion, he adopts an approach that no one in the Bible used at any time, and which certainly wouldn't have occurred to Peter in the context of Acts 15. No one there claimed that if the Gentiles didn't keep the law of Moses they'd suffer from indigestion, ruin their stomachs, and become unhealthy Christians!

Unfortunately, the logic used by Herbert Armstrong is without Biblical basis. He declared the food laws not part of the law of Moses simply on his own authority. He then dictated that we ought to keep them because they're good for our bodies, *and that's that*! On the strength of his dogmatic arguments, coupled with his compelling literary style, tens of thousands of true believers, myself included, accepted this without protest.

The article continues, "Now the eating of wrong food is not a transgression of this spiritual law....It is not necessarily a spiritual sin."[5] "Not necessarily"? That is a strange way to talk about sin, isn't it? Just what does this mean? Is it a sin to eat such food or not? Herbert Armstrong addresses this by saying, "It may not be a spiritual sin to eat biblically unclean foods. Yet, if one deliberately does it out of lust of appetite, that breaks the tenth commandment and it becomes sin."[6] Thus the loop is closed. What begins not as spiritual sin, but merely "physical sin," proves in the end to be real sin after all because of lusting after something wrong.

The article concludes by turning the consumption of "wrong food" into spiritual defilement, "But in all events wrong food injures the body which is the temple of the Holy Spirit. It defiles the BODY if not the *man*, and if we defile our bodies God will destroy us" (I Cor. 3:17).[7]

In other words, eating unclean meats defiles one's body and therefore one's *self*. Contrast this with Christ's own words, "There is *nothing* that enters a man from outside which can defile him" (Mark 7:15). Mr. Armstrong, however, insists that food defiles the body and makes one's body, *one's person or self*, an unfit "temple" for the Holy Spirit. That, for the Christian, elevates food to the highest possible level, for according to Romans 8:9, anyone who does not have the Spirit of God and of Christ, "is not His"— in other words, not saved and not a Christian! That's about as defiled as one can be, isn't it?

Jesus, however, said just the opposite, "Are you without understanding also? Do you not perceive that whatever enters a man from outside cannot defile him because it does not enter his heart but his stomach...?" (Mark 7:18-19). In so saying Jesus removed food from the list of things that cause defilement. He said, "What comes out of a man, that defiles a man. For from within, out of the heart of men, proceed evil thoughts, adulteries, fornications, murders, thefts...All these evil things come from within and defile a man" (verses 20-22).

It becomes obvious that Herbert Armstrong's reasoning is not a sound Biblical treatment of the subject of the food laws. It wins its support by inventing an extra-Biblical law, language, and logic. Worst of all, it contradicts the words and teachings of Jesus Christ.

Let's notice now how Paul introduces the subject of unclean food, "I know and *am convinced by the Lord Jesus* that there is nothing unclean of itself" (Rom. 14:14). Paul appealed to the teaching of the Lord Jesus who earlier challenged and rescinded food as a cause of ritual defilement. Paul fully understood the implications of Jesus' teaching and spelled them out clearly to the Corinthians, "Food does not commend us to God" (I Cor. 8:9), a belief that earlier in his life as a Pharisee, Paul, then Saul, would have firmly resisted.

Herbert Armstrong promised his readers "the New Testament teaching" on food, but sadly, they received *nothing but the Old Testament teaching* and the erroneous notion of "physical sin" (which later turns into *spiritual* sin!) and the declaration, on his own authority, that the food laws are not part of the Mosaic law—something no competent Biblical scholar or authority would support. Members were told that certain foods could defile their bodies and make them unfit for the Holy Spirit, and therefore a people God would destroy! I think we can see clearly now that is *not* the New Testament teaching on food!

Let me tell you, dear reader, it is not easy for me to say these things, and it gives me no pleasure to do so. For one thing, it's embarrassing to see clearly now how cult-like and recklessly authoritarian these "private interpretations" of Scripture really were (II Peter 1:2). I take no pleasure in revealing these doctrinal errors, but I am compelled to do so to be true to the words of Jesus Christ.

We all need to know *where* Herbert Armstrong was wrong, *why* he was wrong, and *how* we were misled. The approach he used in this important Bible subject led to falsehood and error. Herbert Armstrong often *said*, "Don't believe me—believe your Bible." But what he often *did*, in fact, as we see here, was appeal to his own reasoning, his own "proof," and his own authority quite apart from what the Bible says.

If you are still troubled by this issue and wonder what it all means and where it may lead, will you please do this? Will you please allow that obedience to something called "the law of Moses" is not necessary for salvation, despite what you may have believed or practiced over the years? Perhaps you should take a moment to pray about it, asking God to reveal what these scriptures mean and how they should be understood in the light of his Word. The Bible plainly teaches that the law of Moses is not binding or required for salvation or church membership. If you are still struggling with the law-is-required-for-salvation paradigm, ask God the Father and Jesus Christ, who determine the terms and conditions for salvation, to help you gain a fuller Biblical understanding of this vital issue.

Notice the Apostle Paul's astute observation in II Corinthians 3:15, "... even to this day, when Moses is read, a veil covers their hearts." That's still true today. Many have great difficulty accepting the truth about the law of Moses. "But," Paul continues, "whenever anyone turns to the Lord, the veil is taken away."

Chapter Four

Peter's Response
to the Demands of the
Jewish Christians

Let us now examine the response of the apostles and elders at Jerusalem to the demands of the Jewish Christians.

After what Luke calls "much dispute," Peter stood up in their midst, addressed them as "men and brethren," and began his refutation with two very telling words, "You know...." (Acts 15:7). Peter appealed to a prior history of the subject that everyone already knew, namely, the conversion of the Gentiles that began with Peter and Cornelius. By implication, the sense is, "You already know..." and "You should know...." The issue already had been raised, and as far" as Peter was concerned, already had been settled by God. It is as though Peter felt they should know better than to bring up the subject again.

What did they know? "...that a good while ago God chose among us, that by my mouth the Gentiles should hear the word of the gospel and believe" (v.7). Here, Peter reiterates his credentials and states his authority to speak on this subject. As Peter points out to the assembly, God chose him first to take the gospel to the Gentiles and that was now "some time ago," about a decade prior to these events. In other words, this was not a new or novel issue, though some were trying to make it so.

The manner in which Gentiles were added to the Church had been settled, and rather dramatically so, by God himself. That some were trying to contend with this seems, by the tone of his argument, to be more than a little irritating to Peter.

Peter goes straight to the heart of the argument stating, "So *God*, who knows the heart, acknowledged them, by giving them the Holy Spirit just as He did to us" (v. 8). Peter begins with what God has already done to and for the Gentiles, something that should have settled the argument for once and for all. God acknowledged the Gentiles by giving them the Holy Spirit, and confirmed it, as on the first Pentecost, through the miracle of tongues. "And when Peter was still speaking these words (to the household of Cornelius and their friends [Acts 10:24]) the Holy Spirit fell upon all those who heard the word, *and those of the circumcision who believed were astonished*, as many as came with Peter, because the gift of the Holy Spirit had been poured out on the Gentiles also" (Acts 10:44-45).

Peter is reminding the conference that the conversion of the first Gentiles happened in the presence of a good many circumcised, Jewish Christians, much to their amazement, and without any special legal or Mosaic proscriptions, least of all circumcision! And that *they all had known this* for some time.

Peter asserts that God "*made no distinction between us and them*, purifying their hearts by faith" (v.9). Some wanted to make a great distinction between Jewish and Gentile Christians. They considered the new Gentile converts inferior, "second-class citizens," if you will, not entitled to salvation because they weren't circumcised and didn't keep the law of Moses. Peter reminds the assembly that God had, from the beginning, made no such distinction.

Cornelius and his band received the Spirit by faith, as *un*circumcised men, without prior Mosaic instruction or additional requirements. In fact, it was *Peter*, not Cornelius, who had to receive instruction! And that, as we know, came in the form of Peter's vision.

Later, we will discuss Peter's vision in depth, but let's defer that task for now to complete Peter's argument. His words, drawn from the Scripture itself, could hardly be more indicting: "Now *why do you test God?*" (v.10, NIV, NKJV, etc.).

Testing God was the sin Israel committed at Marah that kept them from entering the Promised Land (Exodus 15:22-27). Sadly, Israel persisted in this by challenging God's ability to provide water (Exodus 17:1-7). God repeatedly demonstrated his willingness to deliver Israel with miraculous signs and wonders, yet they stubbornly doubted God's concern for their welfare. This provocation against God is reiterated in Psalm 95, and later described by Paul as a hardened and faithless attitude (Hebrews 3).

Israel of old incessantly tested God's patience and challenged his providence. They chose to "forget" the miracles God repeatedly performed and disbelieved his faithful promise to take care of them. Thus, "testing God" is a term from the Old Testament that describes a faithless, ungrateful, and challenging attitude—a *sin* that was later expressly forbidden in the Law (see Deut. 6:16).

You'll recall that Jesus referred to this command in his defense against Satan in the temptation in the wilderness. Satan challenged Jesus to throw himself off the Temple to force the hand of God to save him. But Jesus declared that to test God violated the law (Luke 4:12).

In Acts 15 Peter invokes this historically powerful language to refute what the legalists were trying to do. The matter of enjoining Mosaic requirements on Gentile converts had been settled long ago, and to revive it now, as though God had not already spoken, was a challenging affront to God himself. God clearly intended to pour out his Holy Spirit unconditionally upon the Gentiles, and had confirmed his intention with signs and miracles. "Why are you challenging God's decision?" Peter demands.

For those of us who would try to do the same today, it should strike fear in our hearts to add requirements for salvation and church membership that God himself does not require! What? Shall we make ourselves holier than God and expect a higher standard of new believers than God himself? If we do, we stand in danger of testing God! This is a serious matter, and we dare not be glib, casual *or stubborn* about it!

Despite this already serious charge, Peter has yet to place the capstone on his argument. He concludes by charging the Jewish Christians with "...putting a yoke on the neck of the disciples which neither our fathers nor we were able to bear" (v.10). Peter likens circumcision and the law of Moses to a yoke, a device that binds an animal to a burden. It is the same language Paul uses in Galatians 5:1 where he proclaims Christian freedom from Mosaic regulation with these stirring words, "Stand fast therefore in the liberty by which Christ has made us free, and do not be entangled again with a *yoke of bondage.* "What is this yoke that no one is able to bear?" asks Kistemaker,

> Obviously, it is the Mosaic law. The Jews
> defined God's law as 'the yoke' which every Jew
> and proselyte had to bear willingly and joyfully.
> Even Jesus uses Jewish imagery when he invites
> those who are weary and burdened to take his yoke
> upon themselves but he tells them that his yoke is
> easy and his burden is light (Matt.11:2-30).[1]

Much more could be said of the light yoke of Jesus, but suffice it to say, for now, that *true Christianity works and works well without all the rules and regulations God enjoined upon Israel through Moses.* No one can know that better than one who has borne the yoke of Moses. Legalists will vigorously insist that they do not find the yoke of the law burdensome—which I suppose means they must be more spiritual than Peter who, after all, "lived in the manner of Gentiles" (Galatians 2:14). Unfortunately, legalists often are blind to the downside effects of legalism and devastating toll it can take.

Be assured for now that yoke means yoke, and that it is for good reason that Paul, inspired by God, warns us not to be encumbered by it. Circumcision and dietary restrictions are no longer a matter of *law* but of *choice*:

> Christ's removal of the yoke of the law made circumcision and kosher eating, etc., no longer obligatory in any sense...yet neither were these Jewish practices and modes of living forbidden by Christ. They became adiaphora, matters of liberty and choice, that should not be forced on others *or become a cause of pride and marks of special holiness as compared with Gentile Christians.* [2]

It will later remain for the Apostle Paul in passages like Romans 14 to explain to the Church in greater detail the workings of Christian liberty in matters of choice. But at this point in the story, Peter has routed the legalists and revealed how wrong-headed and wrong-hearted they were. Yet, he has one more point to make. "But we believe that through the grace of the Lord Jesus Christ we shall be saved in the same manner as they" (Acts 15:11, NKJV).

The NIV translates this verse, "No! We believe it is through the grace of our Lord Jesus that we are saved, just as they are."

Note the sense captured by the NIV: We Jewish Christians *are* saved. Gentile Christians, Peter explains, *are* saved, and have been saved, for years. The church wasn't waiting for the revelation of a new formula for salvation, and none would be forthcoming from this conference. Peter was saying, in effect, *this matter was already decided by God.* All he and the others could do was to accept God's will: *salvation is by the grace of the Lord Jesus Christ to Jew and Gentile alike, with no Mosaic additions.*

It is needless today to resurrect a debate that was adjudicated during the first few decades of the New Testament church. God himself has closed the discussion, and no matter how much some would like to deliberate the issue, no one in the Christian era has ever been given the authority to require the law of Moses of new converts. The Worldwide Church of God at one time did assume such authority, was subsequently corrected of its error, and today, thanks be to God, continues to stand corrected in the light of his Word. It has cost the church dearly in terms of members and support, but that, perhaps, is the price of repentance. Compared to the consequences for tempting God, it is indeed a small price to pay.

In rehearsing the history of these doctrinal errors in the Worldwide Church of God, please be assured that I am not questioning anyone's sincerity, conversion or standing with God. *All churches have doctrinal errors.* And *all ministers make mistakes.* As James said, as ministers and teachers, "We *all* stumble in many things" (James 3:2).

I do not mean to make the mistake of "throwing the baby out with the bath water" and conclude that everything in our past was false and wrong. We had and we still have many precious truths from God that have stood the test of time and need no correcting. We also had mistakes, some of which were by no means minor. But by God's grace, we are dealing with them in the light of his Word, and that's what counts.

Chapter Five

Peter's Vision:
Unclean Meats & Unclean Men

Having heard Peter's inspired response to the Jewish Christians, let's go back for a moment and review the events in Peter's life that prepared him to defend the liberty of the Gentile Christians at the Jerusalem Conference. Recall that Peter is described as the "first" apostle (Matt. 10:2).

Whether acknowledging Jesus as the Son of the living God, walking on water, or whacking off the ear of the high priest's servant, Peter could always be found at the forefront of the action. Once converted, God used Peter's zeal and natural leadership to inspire and strengthen the brethren (Luke 22:32). Christ's commission was to "all nations,"—to Jews and Gentiles alike—(Matt. 28:19), and in Acts 15 we find how God prepared Peter to introduce the gospel to the Gentile world. Just as he had addressed the "men of Israel" and "the house of Israel" on Pentecost (Acts 2:22, 36), Peter was the first apostle to preach to the Gentiles and later taught the whole church how to fulfill this part of its commission.

Curiously, the dream recorded in Acts 10 is called "Peter's vision," yet it begins with a vision to Cornelius, the Roman centurion of the Italian Regiment. A Gentile, to be sure, but not just *any* Gentile—a Gentile of the occupying armies of Rome. But Cornelius was an unusual soldier. Although he served in Caesar's army, he was also "a devout

61

man who feared God with all his household, who gave alms generously to the people, and prayed to God always" (Acts 10:1). It is this pious Italian centurion to whom an angel is sent telling him to send for Peter at Joppa. Under different circumstances, it would not be hard to imagine these men taking up arms against each another, even to the death—Peter, the nationalistic patriot so eager to draw the sword, and Cornelius, a captain in the army of the hated foreign oppressors. However, the historic meeting that occurred between these two dynamic men was destined to change salvational history.

Peter's vision begins not with men but with animals, *all kinds of animals, clean and unclean,* coming down from heaven. A voice instructs him, "Rise, Peter; kill and eat" (Acts 10:13). It's important to note that prior to his trance, Peter was famished and anxiously awaiting the noon meal. Despite his great hunger, Peter's instinctive response, *even though he knows he is speaking to God*, is to exclaim, "Not so, Lord!" (v.14).

Amazing! This is the same man who, when bid by Jesus to come to him on the water, stepped right out of the boat and did so without hesitation. But when it came to life-long prohibitions about food, he vehemently defied Christ himself!

Peter was not the first to do so nor the last. Ezekiel said much the same thing when asked to prepare his food using human waste for fuel (Ezek. 4:14, NIV), and some are still refusing God's instruction saying, in their own way, "Not so, Lord!".

But why Peter's staunch refusal to obey the voice of God? The next four words in verse 14 explain: "For I have *never....*" This command from the Lord was just too strange, too different. It ran contrary to the whole of Peter's personal, cultural, and religious experience. He was being commanded to do something he had *never* done before and could not bring himself to do now, even though the Lord was telling him to do it.

And what was this command that Peter found harder to perform than walking on water? Eating formerly forbidden unclean food, "I have never eaten anything common or unclean" (v.14). Peter couldn't bring himself to violate his conscience and one of the strongest cultural prohibitions of the Jewish world. So strong was his revulsion that, even in a dream, the usually impulsive Peter chose to disobey God rather than change his diet!

He is rebuked for his obstinacy by the voice he knows is the Lord's, "What God has cleansed you must not call common" (v.15) Why does the Lord insist that Peter eat? Let's understand this properly. Peter is told he must no longer think of these animals as unclean *because God has declared them clean*.

What is going on here? Is the voice from heaven telling Peter to sin? To do evil? To violate the commands of God? That would be a strange command from heaven! And is the reason given permitting him to eat—that the animals are no longer unclean—the truth or a lie? Are the animals really cleansed or not?

I raise these questions because according to former Worldwide Church of God doctrine, we were taught that the vision only concerned human beings and had nothing whatever to do with food or animals. The principal intent of the vision, I realize, is that Peter is to accept the Gentile believers. But how are we to understand the vision itself? Why would God *command* Peter to sin by eating unclean meat—even *symbolically*—and then *lie* about having "cleansed" the meat? If this is, indeed, only to be understood symbolically and not literally, why would God use *unclean and impure animals* to symbolize *cleansed people*? If so, what kind of symbolism is that? If God is "not really serious" about cleansing the animals, how can Peter be sure he's really "serious" about cleansing the Gentiles? Perhaps one of our church's most oft-quoted scriptures can be aptly applied here—"God is not the author of confusion!" (1 Cor. 14:33).

The far plainer and simpler explanation, of course, is that Jesus is giving Peter a legitimate command as well as a valid reason for administering that command. The Lord was simply telling Peter to eat food that, though previously forbidden, he had now declared edible and clean. Why should that come as any surprise to Peter or to us? Is this not God's prerogative?

We are told that after the Flood God gave Noah and his descendants permission to eat of all the animals, "*Every moving thing that lives* shall be food for you" (Gen.9:3). (Or must we make that another "difficult scripture" and somehow convince ourselves it does not mean what it says?)

Later, in the days of Moses and Israel, God made a new law concerning animal flesh, "This is the law of the beasts and every living creature...to distinguish between the unclean and the clean" (Lev. 11:4;6-47). This is God's prerogative. By his own power and authority he can forbid or allow things of a physical or ceremonial nature. Food is a *physical matter*, and please let's not try to make it more than that. (To be sure, God does not treat intrinsically moral and spiritual matters such as lying, murder or adultery in this way, as we shall see later.)

Still later, at a different time and for different reasons, God removed the clean/unclean distinction, and reestablished the mandate given to Noah. Paul taught the New

Testament church, "*Every creature of God is good,* and *nothing is to be refused* if it is received with thanksgiving" (I Tim.4:4). The food laws, and their reasons for being, have changed over time as God has dealt with his people, as have other laws of a physical nature such as circumcision. Nevertheless, Peter was fettered, like many today, by a paradigm that had outlived its usefulness and was, in fact, no longer in effect.

Once *properly* understood, the symbolism of Peter's vision makes perfect sense! *Formerly* unclean animals, now cleansed, are symbolic of *formerly* unclean human beings, now also cleansed. The best explanations, I'm sure you'll agree, are almost always the simplest.

"The voice conveys the message that God, who formulated the dietary laws for his people Israel, can also revoke them according to his sovereign will," Kistemaker explains. "God has made the animals clean; therefore, Peter with his fellow Jewish Christians can disregard the food laws that have been observed since the days of Moses."[1] That is, to quote a familiar phrase, "the plain truth" about Peter's vision!

Food law disputes were part of the deep rift between the Jewish and Gentiles Christians. In the past, the clean/unclean meat distinctions were intended to keep Israel separate from the other nations. But now God was proclaiming a universal gospel of salvation to *all* nations, and it was time for the dietary restrictions, with their inevitable social barriers, to come to an end.

"When does God abolish the dietary laws for Jewish Christians?" asks Kistemaker,

The moment God removes the barrier between Jew and Gentile, the validity of the food laws ceases. Abolition of these laws means that Jewish and Gentile Christians enter a new relationship and accept one another as equals in the church. God himself removes the barrier, for he is the lawmaker. [2]

Peter was a little slow to catch on, it's true, but old habits die hard, especially when they are reinforced by powerful cultural norms. The Jews of Peter's day understood that the food laws were intended to prohibit potentially corrupting social contact with Gentiles. This mind-set explains why Peter said to Cornelius, "You know how unlawful it is for a Jewish man to keep company with or go to one of another nation" (Acts 10:28).

The dietary restrictions and other "holiness laws" effectively kept the Jews separated from other nations. Unfortunately, they had the same effect in the early church. And despite his wholehearted defense of the Gentiles in Acts 10, Peter, ironically, was later rebuked by Paul for refusing to eat with the Gentile brethren, "For before certain men came from James, he would eat with the Gentiles; but when they came, he withdrew and separated himself, fearing those who were of the circumcision" (Gal. 2:12). Hard to believe, isn't it, that Peter could understand the meaning of his vision and explain it to the household of Cornelius, and then later refuse to eat with Gentiles in the presence of the Jewish brethren.

Paul, on the other hand, seems to have had an easier time internalizing the changes in the food laws, and on this awkward occasion actually chose to withstand Peter to his face (Gal. 2:11). F. F. Bruce in his New Testament Commentary explains,

As for Paul, he took a different line...No food, he maintained was 'common or unclean' per se—not even if it had been forbidden by the law of Moses, not even if it came from an animal that had been sacrificed to a pagan divinity. *It was human beings that mattered, not food.*[3]

Paul in his writings made it clear that food is a matter of personal liberty, not Biblical command. Let's look at five examples:

1. "For one believes that he may eat *all things*, but he who is weak in the faith eats only vegetables. Let not him who eats despise him who does not eat, and let him who does not eat judge him who eats" (Rom. 14:2-3).

2. "I know and am convinced by the Lord Jesus that there is *nothing unclean of itself*, but to him who considers anything to be unclean, to him it is unclean...*The kingdom of God is not food and drink*, but righteousness and peace, and joy in the Holy Spirit" (Rom. 14:14-17).

3. *"But food does not commend us to God*; for neither if we eat are we better, nor if we do not eat are we worse" (I Cor. 8:8).

4. "Some will depart from the faith...forbidding to marry and commanding to abstain from food which God has created to be received with thanksgiving by those who know and believe the truth. For every creature of God is good and nothing to be refused if it is received with thanksgiving" (I Tim 4:3-4).

5.   "Do not be carried about with various and strange doctrines. *For it is good that the heart be established by grace, not with foods* which have not profited those who have been occupied with them," or as the Phillips' translates it so clearly, "Spiritual stability depends on the grace of God, and not on rules of diet—which after all have not spiritually benefitted those who have made a specialty of that kind of thing" (Heb. 13:9).

This is a good example of the principle, "two are better than one" (Eccl. 4:9). Peter was the first to receive Christ's new instruction, but accepted it with some difficulty. Paul, as the apostle to the Gentiles, apparently grasped the principle immediately and consistently applied it. To reiterate F.F. Bruce's summation, "It was human beings that mattered, not food."

The foods laws proved a barrier to fellowship in the gospel that God then removed. Note that, "Even though some Gentiles worship with the Jews in the local synagogue, they are unable to socialize with them because of the Jewish laws on table fellowship."[4] Amazing! You could worship with your Gentile proselyte "brother" on the Sabbath at the synagogue but because of the food laws you could not have dinner with him at his house or yours on Saturday night!

Members of the Worldwide Church of God will not have a problem identifying with this, for in times past they, too, avoided places, activities, and events where they might find themselves having to deal with "clean and unclean meats."

Sadly, this even included family get-togethers. On other occasions they might attend such a function but have to decline the "unclean food" much to everyone's awkwardness and embarrassment. Herbert Armstrong openly admitted that, while dining with dignitaries and heads of state, to avoid being offensive or rude, he ate what was set before him "asking no question for conscience sake." Most members, however, did not feel free to do so, and many a minister would have frowned on such a practice.

This is a good example of the law of Moses as a yoke of bondage. We in the church often put food before fellowship and caused unnecessary hurt and offense to family and friends.

> "Hear Me, everyone and understand:
> *There is nothing that enters a man from outside which can defile him*; but the things which come out of him, those are the things that defile a man. If anyone has ears to hear, let him hear!" (Mark 7:14-16).

Those are Christ's own words! I hope we all have ears to hear him and do not refuse by saying, "Not so, Lord!"

Difficult Scriptures

Chapter Six

James' Counsel to the Gentiles

Peter's forceful discourse recounting God's acceptance of the Gentiles apart from any Mosaic requirements gave those at the Jerusalem Conference a sound basis for a decision. But as far as Peter was concerned, the problem *had been resolved a decade earlier* and required no novel solution. Peter sternly warned against brazenly testing or tempting God on a matter which, in his sovereignty, He had decided, once and for all.

I say this so we can properly understand the Apostle James' subsequent role at the Jerusalem Conference. Unfortunately the familiar phrase from the Authorized Text, "Wherefore my sentence is..." (Acts 15:9, KJV) has been taken by many to mean that it was James who made the final decision. This, as we'll see, is a wrong presumption and assigns to James a role he never claimed and a meaning he never intended.

James was highly respected as an apostle, brother of the Lord, and pastor of the Jerusalem church, but scripture nowhere assigns him—nor does he ever claim—authority over either Peter or Paul. He was neither a judge, nor a lawgiver, as was Moses. He was, however, a wise and respected church leader who sagely and skillfully addressed the assembly on the matter at hand.

Notice his tactful, opening remark, "Simon has declared how God at first visited the Gentiles..." (Acts 15:14). Using Peter's Hebrew name was a diplomatic way of alleviating the tension emanating from the restive Jewish contingent present at the counsel. "Simon has declared..." also acknowledges Peter's precedent-setting experience concerning the conversion of the Gentiles. James' definitive choice of words suggests that he both agrees with and defers to Peter on the matter.

But ultimately James reveals he is deferring not to man but to God: "Simon has declared how *God*...." James does not consider himself a central figure in this historic debate, nor does he appropriate to himself the judicial authority to render the final "sentence." Instead, he supports Peter with Scripture, saying, "And with this the words of the prophets agree..." (Acts 15:15-17). That's like saying, "Peter's right, and you can prove it by the Bible."

As an apostle and preeminent church elder, we could expect Peter to be chosen by God to introduce doctrinal change. And for all practical purposes, that is exactly what occurred. "There remained, however, *practical problems*," notes F.F. Bruce.

> In most cities Gentile believers had to live alongside Jewish believers, who had been brought up to observe the levitical food restrictions and to avoid contact with Gentiles as far as possible. If there was to be free association between these two groups, *certain guidelines must be laid down*, especially with regard to table fellowship.[1]

In other words, Peter issued the decision, but the practical applications had yet to be discussed. That neither the law of Moses nor circumcision were required for salvation was now clear to all, but on what basis were Jews and Gentiles to have fellowship? Did any principles apply to their new situation? Were there any guidelines?

James addressed this new state of affairs by offering his considered judgment. "It is my judgment..." is the NIV's treatment of this famous phrase. The text also can be translated "I for my part judge...," a far less officious rendering than, "Wherefore my sentence is..." (a phrase, incidentally, carefully chosen by the King James Version translators to show that Peter was not the "chief apostle," and to diminish the authority of any who claimed to be his successors).

James shares with the assembly his advice, or "considered judgment" as to how the two groups should accommodate one another under the new dispensation. His counsel is thus directed at both parties.

His first recommendation is, "that we should not make it difficult for the Gentiles who are turning to God" (Acts 15:19, NIV). The old rules made fellowship difficult if not impossible, and that had to change.

The Greek phrase here is better translated "Do not annoy..." or more literally, "Do not crowd in on...."

"James regards the Judaistic demands made on the Gentile Christians as crowding these Christians in an uncalled for manner, annoying them without warrant," notes Kistemaker. He adds,

> This is exactly what the Judaizers are doing to the believers: they crowd into the lives of the Gentiles by demanding circumcision and the observance of the Mosaic law. James refrains from mentioning circumcision and obedience to the law, but he employs language that says: 'Stop crowding in on these people.'[2]

Those who have lived under such restrictions know from experience how they can crowd in on one's life and needlessly annoy others. At last we, too, are saying, "Stop crowding in on these people!"

James then tells the Gentile Christians what they can and should do to make amicable fellowship possible, "Abstain from food polluted by idols, from sexual immorality, from the meat of strangled animals and from blood" (Acts 15:20). These are simply reasonable requests made of the Gentiles to avoid offense. They are not, however, the introduction of a new Gentile code of law.

Gentiles were to abstain from foods polluted by idols and the sexual immorality that so commonly accompanied pagan worship (see 1 Cor. 8:7-8, "Do not become idolaters...nor let us commit sexual immorality"), and they were not to eat meat with the blood still in it or eat blood itself. These guidelines were to prevent offense, facilitate fellowship, and promote unity between Jewish and Gentile Christians.

Let us not see them, as some do, as an abbreviated moral catechism or an introduction to a new legal system to replace the one from which the Gentiles were just released. Referring to the last two requests, Lenski comments:

> Why, then, introduce these items? Certainly not in order again to enforce these points of the Levitical law. That would have been Judaistic legalism...James mentions these two points because Jewish Christians were especially sensitive regarding them....The Gentiles Christians were asked to respect this feeling and thus from motives of brotherly love refrain from eating blood and meat that still had its blood.[3]

That kind of careful exposition is in order lest we conclude that one set of legal requirements was lifted by Peter only to be replaced by another from James.

That these were not intended as a new set of divine laws for Gentiles is proven by the fact that at least one of these recommendations, namely, not eating meats offered to or polluted by idols, was all but eliminated later by Paul (I Cor. 8 and 10). Gentiles now were permitted to eat meats polluted by idols if doing so caused no one offense (I Cor. 10:28). Clearly some of these guidelines could be modified if necessary, and when warranted by circumstances such as those Paul faced at Corinth.

The same qualifiers can be applied to James' final counsel, "For Moses has been preached in every city from the earliest times and is read in the synagogues on every sabbath." Contrary to the view held by modern legalists, and although both Moses and the sabbath are mentioned in the same breath, this text cannot be used as proof that Christians today are bound by the law of Moses. Taken in context, James was merely admonishing the Gentiles to be sensitive to the Jewish culture and to accept a few behavioral guidelines that would help keep the peace and avoid offence. The Jews and Gentiles, however, were equally responsible for maintaining a harmonious fellowship. The Jews were to accept the Gentiles unreservedly, and the Gentiles were to refrain from behaviors that the Jews would perceive as repugnant.

Kistemaker summarizes the issues well:

> (James) suggests four recommendations that are applicable to Gentile Christians who associate with Jewish Christians, especially those who live in the dispersion. He seeks to promote unity among believers of both Jewish and Gentile backgrounds. James wants the Christians to live together in wholesome relationships. He desires they observe certain prescribed rules which preclude any offense arising from table fellowship or social contacts.[4]

This brings us close to the end of this pivotal episode in salvational history. What remains is the letter sent to the Gentile Christians summing up the conference's decision, and announcing the decision to the churches at and around Antioch where problem first arose. Paul, Barnabus, and Silas were chosen for this purpose, no doubt because they were commissioned by God to preach in the Gentile regions. They were also the first to oppose the legalistic demands of the Jewish Christians (Acts 15:2).

Thus the story comes full circle—Paul and Barnabus, who were vigorous opponents of legalism from the start, appealed the question to the apostles and elders at Jerusalem, saw legalism rejected, and carried the decision back to their churches.

It sounds almost too simple to be true. Perhaps its been simple all along, but I lived with much confusion on these "simple" matters for many years, and I still see many people deeply confused about them today.

I have tried my best to make Act 15 as plain to you, dear reader, as I can. I hope that you now *know with certainty* that you do not have to keep the law of Moses in order to be saved or to enjoy Christian fellowship.

Chapter Seven

Eat Whatever Is Set Before You

Now that we've reviewed the issues and outcome of the Jerusalem Conference, what, exactly, happened *afterward*? How, in real-life terms, did these decisions "play out" in the churches?

The events we have been discussing occurred about 50 AD. An additional fifteen years, approximately, of church history are recorded in the Acts, up to and including Paul's imprisonment. The Epistles continue beyond the deaths of Peter and Paul, through at least the mid-80's. John, at this point, was the last remaining apostle. Most scholars say he wrote the Book of Revelation in the '90's, while exiled on the Isle of Patmos. From Acts 15 through the Book of Revelation, approximately four decades of church history passed. What happened during those years?

If you assumed that the controversy about foods ceased to be an issue in the church, you would be 100% correct! Yet, those who maintain that the Old Covenant is still in effect would not be inclined to agree. They would be looking for confirmation that the Mosaic law is still in force, believing it can be found in the pages of the New Testament.

What I want to demonstrate in this chapter is that after the Jerusalem Conference in Acts *all the evidence surrounding the food debate points only one way.* Ironically, one Jewish Talmudic scholar has found this surprisingly easy to understand. Hyam Maccoby, writing on Acts 15 from a *Jewish* perspective, discusses exactly what changed,

By the decision of the Jerusalem Counsel, Gentile followers of Jesus were *not* (emphasis his) obliged to keep the Jewish dietary laws, but only to refrain from the meat of 'strangled animals.' This meant that they were allowed to eat the meat of animals forbidden to Jews, e.g., pig and rabbit, but were obliged to kill the animals by the Jewish method, by which the blood was drained away. [1]

Even to someone fully immersed in Jewish orthodoxy, the meaning of Acts 15 and the Counsel of Jerusalem is strikingly clear. Maccoby knows how Jews and Gentiles differ on the matter of food laws and does not minimize or obscure the difference. He quite understands the historic and social context of Acts 15 and spells out the obvious consequences. Many Bible commentators such as Dunn and Kistemaker (quoted elsewhere and oft cited in the references) interpret the evidence similarly and have come to the same conclusions.

What Christians were permitted to eat following the Jerusalem Conference is summed up by Paul, "If any of those who do not believe invites you to dinner, and you desire to go, eat whatever is set before you, asking no question for conscience sake" (I Cor. 10:27).

I am fully aware that the meats in question here are those offered to idols, and that it is debatable whether they were beef, pork, lamb, or shellfish. However, that does not change the comprehensive nature of Paul's statement. You may eat *"whatever"* is set before you and *you are not obligated spiritually* to ask what it is or how it was prepared. Spiritual defilement is not determined by what goes in one's mouth, as Jesus plainly said in the Gospels. Defilement is something that comes from within, not from without.

After the Jerusalem Conference, food was a matter of choice, not a matter of law. As it was after the Flood, and before Sinai, foods were no longer regulated or restricted by law. Earlier, in I Corinthians 10 , Paul wrote, "Eat whatever is sold in the meat market, asking no questions for conscience' sake" (I Cor. 10:25). I still remember our attempts in the Worldwide Church of God to explain this by insisting only clean meats were sold in the Corinthian meat market. Kosher meats in a Gentile meat market? Is that logical?

But, in fact, all of Paul's statements in his epistles are permissive regarding food. None are restrictive—*with one notable exception*—you may eat "all things" *unless* your eating is going to cause offense. Then you must abstain from meat or any food so as not to cause another person to stumble. One ought to abstain, not only from meat, but from *any* "offensive" food. This is made very clear in I Corinthians 10:23-31. But that one exception concerns *people*, not food.

As for food, as we've already seen, Paul said, "There is nothing that is unclean of itself," nothing that defiles a person or makes him unholy in the eyes of God, "Yet if your brother is grieved because of your food, you are no longer walking in love. Do not destroy with your food the one for whom Christ died." And that is the *only* food restriction you will find in the New Testament. After Acts 15, we never again encounter a sermon or a comment on "clean and unclean meat," any mention of someone eating "pork" or "swineflesh," or the slightest hint or suggestion that someone was wrong or condemned in God's sight because of his or her choice of food.

In my experience in the Worldwide Church of God I did hear occasional messages on the food laws or "health laws," as they were often called. I remember giving at least one sermon that focused on distinguishing the clean from the unclean, and of course, I discussed unclean meats. We observed and we enforced the food laws. Pork products were *not* a welcome sight at our church socials, and if a non-member spouse brought bologna sandwiches, coldcuts, or a shrimp salad to a picnic, the offending item would be removed from the table discreetly or probably never put out in the first place. Such foods immediately branded a person as "outside the Church," and hence, unconverted. Contrary to everything taught by Peter, Paul, and Christ himself, food, for years, was one "identifying sign" of a true Christian and member of the Worldwide Church of God.

After Acts 15 the issue of "clean and unclean meats" disappears during the remaining four decades of church history recorded in the New Testament. Neither sacred nor secular history is kind to the legalist looking for proof for this argument. It is simply not there. This lack of evidence should tell us something, because a great many critical spiritual issues do remain in the forefront in the New Testament. Adultery, fornication, and sexual immorality, for example, are discussed at great length. You'll recall in describing "the acts of the sinful nature" (NIV) or "works of the flesh" (NKJV), Paul begins with adultery and fornication (Gal. 5:19). He makes it very plain to the wayward Corinthians what kinds of behaviors will keep a person from inheriting the Kingdom of God—fornication, idolatry, adultery, and homosexuality (I Cor. 6:9).

Some sins are frequently mentioned, especially those that break and destroy relationships. Other things that were formerly considered sins under the law of Moses, such as pork eating, tithe stealing, and sabbath breaking, are not mentioned once. After Acts 15, they simply become *non-issues*.

Over the years and again recently, I have heard an imaginative explanation for this total omission: The reason that those things are never mentioned is that everyone already understood and agreed with all of them, and kept them so perfectly that there was simply no need to bring them up! All the Jews and all those new Gentile converts just "got with the program"—they paid their tithes, avoided the wrong foods, kept all the right days, and did so with such thoroughness and zeal, there was no need for a sermon or word of exhortation or reproof to anyone at any time, ever again.

That's rather ingenious, I have to admit, but it is also farfetched. It is out of touch with the heated debate that dominated the Jerusalem Conference. For such an argument to be valid, the decision of the Conference would have to have been wholesale capitulation to the demands of the Jewish Christians, which of course, did not occur. After having these requirements lifted, is it reasonable to believe that the Gentiles would have somehow re-embraced them without one word of protest or complaint? The far more obvious reason for the deafening silence on all these matters is that when the letter went out to the churches, everyone knew the council's decision and lived by it.

All the subsequent Biblical evidence points one way and one way only. Please, don't take my word for it. Do your own homework and you'll see that there isn't any New Testament or post-apostolic evidence to uphold the Old Covenant food laws. In the mid-60's when Christians were martyred under Nero and in all the dreadful persecutions that followed, devout men and women suffered and died for their faith in Christ, not for their refusal to eat pork, as had the Jews during the reign of Antiochus. The Jews would rather have died than become defiled from eating pork. "Many in Israel stood firm and were resolved in their hearts not to eat unclean food. They chose to die rather that to be defiled by food or to profane the holy covenant; and they did die" (I Macc. 1.60-3).

One has to admire the Covenant faithfulness of those devout Jews. Nevertheless, we never read of Christians dying for their refusal to eat certain foods. They died for their faith in Jesus, not their allegiance to the law of Moses. These facts have enormous implications that all Christians today need to consider.

I chose to begin with a discussion of paradigms and what exceptions mean. The termination of the food regulations God gave to Moses and the children of Israel stands as proof positive that the Old Covenant has come to an end. The collapse of the Mosaic food laws in New Testament is to the whole Mosaic code what the moons of Jupiter are to an earth-centered astronomy—the death of an old paradigm.

The dissolution of the food laws has deeper implications than merely the end of some bothersome dietary restrictions. Along with the abolition of the animal sacrifices and circumcision, they mark the end of a system that dominated the Biblical landscape dating back to the days of Moses. And as we shall see, they are only one of *several* Mosaic requirements that ceased after Acts 15.

Chapter Eight

Are the Annual Festivals
Part of the Law of Moses?

Today, as I write, it is February 29th, 1996, Leap Year Day. It's an unusual and somehow appropriate day on which to begin this section on the Old Testament festivals. As we all know, there is a reason why there is a 29th day in February every four years, and a clear rationale for adding an extra day to the calendar. The solar year is three hundred sixty five and one quarter days long, which means that every four years we gain an extra day—a day which need to be added to the calendar to keep it accurate.

We all accept the need for an extra calendar day every four years and most of us know the rationale for it. But are we equally clear about the rationale for the observance or non-observance of the annual sabbaths? Can we give good, solid reasons for keeping, or not keeping, the Days of Unleavened Bread, Pentecost, the Feast of Trumpets, and the Feast of Tabernacles?

If we insist they must be kept by Christians today, what is our rationale? And by what authority do we make this pronouncement? And if we do not believe these days must be kept, how did we arrive at our conclusion?

To be sure, Leap Year is just a secular matter. There are no spiritual consequences for failure to observe Leap Year. But the annual festivals or "holy days" of the Bible

are a scriptural matter which would have spiritual consequences if they are required. We need to have solid, Biblical
reasons for keeping them, or not.

The key issue is whether they are binding and obligatory
for Christians today. Are they required for salvation? A related
issue is, what makes them binding or not binding; that is, what
is the source of their authority?

Clearly, the source of authority for the annual festivals is
not the Ten Commandments for there is no mention of
them there. One may argue that the weekly sabbath derives
its authority from the Ten Commandments, but one cannot
use the same argument for the annual sabbaths.

What, then, is the source of their authority?
Anyone who insists on observing the annual sabbaths must
at some point come to grips with these questions: Are
the annual festivals part of the law of Moses? and *do
the annual sabbaths derive their authority from the law
of Moses?*

To his credit, Herbert Armstrong was familiar with those
questions and did face them squarely. Where he did and how he did
will be discussed in considerable detail in the pages that follow.

But let's stay with these questions long enough to
recognize their implications. If the only source of
authority for observing the annual sabbaths is the law of
Moses, and if, as we have seen, the law of Moses is not
binding or required of Christians today, then it follows that
there is no binding authority for their observance.

Herbert Armstrong knew this to be true and therefore
went to great lengths to assure his readers that the annual
sabbaths or "holy days," as we in the Worldwide Church
of God usually called them, were emphatically *not*
part of the law of Moses. He was from the very beginning eager to establish the authority for these days

apart from the law of Moses and the Old Covenant. He knew that if they were a part of either, they would not be binding on Christians today.

Before we analyze Mr. Armstrong's arguments, let me ask you what you think about this matter. Have you given it much thought? Do you think the annual sabbaths or festivals are part of the law of Moses or not? Do they derive their authority from the law of Moses or not? Can anyone insist that Christians today must observe them because they are required for salvation?

As we'll see in detail, Herbert Armstrong tried to prove, as he did with the dietary laws, that the annual sabbaths *are not* part of the law of Moses. My premise in this chapter is that the annual festivals *are* clearly a part of the law of Moses—as much a part of that legal package as are the dietary laws. I will argue throughout this chapter and the rest of this book that Christians are at liberty to keep these days, and will allow that there may be benefits and advantages in so doing. But I will also demonstrate, as I did for the dietary laws, that they were and are part of the Old Covenant, and as such are no longer binding.

I'll discuss all of Herbert Armstrong's proofs, then give you mine, and you can decide for yourself which you find more convincing. "Prove all things; hold fast what is good," God commands (I Thess. 5:21, (KJV). And to rework a familiar phrase—"Don't believe *either of us*; believe your Bible!"

For Mr. Armstrong's perspective on the annual festivals, I'll be citing his booklet <u>Pagan Holidays—or God's Holy Days—Which?</u>. That is the booklet which, over the years, convinced tens of thousands of members of the Worldwide Church of God to observe the annual festivals, myself included.

The very first notion Mr. Armstrong tries to put to rest is that the annual sabbaths are part of the law of Moses. Under the subtitle, "Study This Twice," he writes, "Such arguments as 'The annual Sabbaths are part of the law of Moses'...*are not Scriptural*" (emphasis mine).[1]

Mr. Armstrong seems very much aware that there are those who would contend that the annual festivals *are* part of the law of Moses, and takes special pains at the outset to declare this argument unscriptural. A page or two later he cites Leviticus 23, the chapter in which all the annual sabbaths are described. Ironically, he locates the festivals within a book which, probably more than any other, is regarded as *the* definitive explication of the law of Moses, yet he dogmatically states that these festivals are not part of that law!

How can he do this? Everyone knows that the festivals began in the days of Moses, are found in the books of Moses, and are part of the law given through Moses to the children of Israel. How can he so confidently declare them to be otherwise?

Here's how! Mr. Armstrong writes, "For the annual sabbaths were NOT part of the law of Moses, but were observed before the ritualistic ordinances contained in the law of Moses were given."[2] That's how he begins distancing the annual festivals from the law of Moses—by stating they were observed before what he calls "the ritualistic ordinances" of the Mosaic law were given.

As we saw in Chapter Three, in order to dislodge the dietary regulations from the law of Moses, Mr. Armstrong invented a new category of law he called "Basic Law." That was his device for rescuing the food laws from their origins in the law of Moses.

Here, too, he uses an eccentric device to pull the annual festivals out of the law of Moses and establish their authority by some other means. He simply says they were observed *before* the law of Moses. It's an argument based on time, on precedent, on priority. We will examine the merits of that argument very carefully.

Another device he employs is to minimize the breadth of the Mosaic law. In the aforementioned quotation, he implies that the law of Moses was composed primarily of "ritualistic ordinances" and did not include commandments, statutes (the Holy Days are statutes) or judgments. Here, from the same page, is Mr. Armstrong's working definition of the law of Moses,

> The law of Moses contained those ritualistic or ceremonial laws which were ADDED, because of transgressions of the Old Covenant, added until Christ—to teach and instill into them the HABIT of obedience. These consisted of meat and drink offerings, various washings, physical ordinances. Also they had the SACRIFICES, as a substitute for the sacrifice of Christ (emphasis his). [3]

So the argument "proving" that the annual festivals are not part of the law of Moses is that they existed before the law of Moses and that the law of Moses is really only a matter of rituals, ceremonies, and sacrifices.

I would urge you at this point to review the second chapter of this book, "Biblically Defining the Law of Moses," to see if this narrow definition of the law of Moses harmonizes with the dozens of references cited there. Remember that Ezra's reading of "the Book of the

Law of Moses" resulted in the observance of the Feast of Tabernacles (Neh. 8:1, 13-18). Recall, too, that according to I Kings 2:3, the law of Moses includes "His statutes, His commandments, His judgments, and His testimonies," and not just "ritualistic ordinances."

Herbert Armstrong is pleased to quote Leviticus 23 in support of the annual festivals. Did he think of Leviticus as somehow *not* part of the law of Moses? Many would say that of all of the books of the Pentateuch that could be called law of Moses, surely Leviticus would be one. But as noted earlier, there was really no place in Worldwide Church of God theology for the law of Moses.

According to this narrow and highly individualistic view of the law of Moses, it had to remain a vague and obscure collection of "ritualistic or ceremonial laws." It could include meat and drink offerings, washings, and mere physical ordinances, but in Mr. Armstrong's scheme of things, surely nothing as important as dietary or festival laws.

Clearly, it is Herbert Armstrong's narrow interpretation of the law of Moses that is unscriptural. While it may perhaps serve the needs of his argument, his definition does not align with the much broader Old Testament or New Testament applications.

And if not in Leviticus, where in the Bible *is* the law of Moses to be found? In what specific books or passages, then, is it defined? In Worldwide Church of God theology we always seemed to treat the law of Moses as some shadowy, ill-defined, hard-to-locate portion of the Scripture. No one seemed to know for sure *where* it was!

In <u>Pagan Holidays—or God's Holy Days—Which?</u> we find the discussion "Prior to the Law of Moses," in which Mr. Armstrong asserts that the annual Holy Days were observed prior to Sinai. Is there evidence that these festivals were observed before the law of Moses was given? Do you know? I think you will find this interesting.

Admittedly, it would be a convincing argument if it could be demonstrated that Adam, Seth, Enoch, and Noah, and/or Abraham, Isaac, and Jacob, observed the annual festivals. Indeed, it would show that these days did not stem from the Old Covenant. We would have a powerful precedent for keeping the annual sabbaths quite apart from Moses. But can this be proven from the Bible? No, it cannot, because it is not there. But notice what Mr. Armstrong actually meant by "prior to."

> In the 12th chapter of Exodus, while the Children of Israel were still in Egypt— long before any of the law of Moses had been given—prior to the time when God revealed to Moses and the Israelites He would make the Old Covenant with them—we find God's annual holy days being observed.[4]

So what does Mr. Armstrong mean by "prior to the Law of Moses?" He means Israel's observance of the first Passover on the night of the Exodus and the sabbath that immediately followed (the first Day of Unleavened Bread). That's it! That constitutes his whole proof that the annual festivals are not part of the law of Moses.

Note carefully that this Holy Day observance is supposed to have been "long before" the law of Moses. But just how "long before" the giving of the law was that first Passover? It is generally understood that Moses received the law on Pentecost, and Pentecost comes, of course, fifty days after the weekly sabbath within the Days of Unleavened Bread. So "long before" actually turns out to be *less than two months*! Can a period of less than eight weeks truly be considered "long before"?

Clearly, the "long before" argument would be compelling if one could find scriptural evidence that the Holy Days were observed by Adam, Noah, or Abraham. But only a few short weeks separate the giving of the law at Sinai and the observance of the first Passover and Days of Unleavened Bread. From a historical perspective, these are contemporaneous events. They are all of the same time frame, woven of the same historical cloth. The Exodus is not, in practical fact, "long before" the giving of the law at Sinai.

Mr. Armstrong continues, "And in the 23rd chapter of Leviticus we find a summary of these annual Holy Days or set feasts." After dismissing the law of Moses in one paragraph, he leaps back into it in the next!

The two passages he uses to support his premise are Exodus 12 and Leviticus 23. Let's turn to these verses; notice how they begin:

"And the Lord spoke to Moses and Aaron in the land of Egypt saying..." (Ex. 12:1).

"And the Lord spoke to Moses saying..." (Lev. 23:1).

What we find in these verses is a statement or a formula that is used over 100 times in Exodus, Leviticus, and Numbers. Take the time to examine for yourself how many chapters and major sub-sections of these books begin with this phrase.

Note Exodus 10:1, 11:1, 12:1, 13:1, 14:1, and Leviticus 1:1, 4:1, 6:1, 8:1, and the first verses of chapters 11-26. These verses all begin with, "And the Lord spoke to Moses saying." This phrase is the first part of a two-part formula we read over and over again in these books.

The second part of this formula is found in Exodus 12:3, "Speak to all the congregation of Israel saying..." and Leviticus 23:2, "Speak to the children of Israel and say to them..."

What is occurring here? God speaks to Moses and then Moses speaks to the children of Israel, commanding them to observe the Passover and Days of Unleavened Bread. Why is this significant? Clearly, Moses is God's spokesperson to Israel. He is called "the mediator" of the Old Covenant (Gal. 3:19.) In Exodus 3 God selects Moses for this role. Moses balks at the responsibility, so God appoints his brother Aaron as a helper (Ex. 3-4).

With this background in mind, let us now ask ourselves whether the events in Exodus 12 are proof positive that the annual festivals cannot be part of the law of Moses. Did the Passover instructions God gave to Israel through Moses occur substantially *prior to*, or were they significantly *different from* the statements made in Leviticus 23? Read it for yourself; they are not at all appreciably different, nor are they separated by enough time to prove they are not part of the Mosaic law.

These Scriptures are talking about the *same* person— Moses, who is talking to the *same* people—Israel, in the *same* season of the *same* year, using the *same* formula to give almost the *same* commands concerning the *same* festivals. In both Exodus 12 and Leviticus 23 God commands the children of Israel through Moses to observe the Passover and Days of Unleavened Bread. Another law, the law of the firstborn is also given at this time (Ex. 13:2).

Herbert Armstrong did not in fact establish that the annual festivals pre-date the law of Moses. Rather, in Exodus 12 God reveals, *for the first time*, his laws concerning these festivals. They are reiterated in Leviticus 23, Exodus 23, are Numbers 28. *All of these passages* are part of the law of Moses.

God's laws concerning the annual sabbaths, and a great many other things, came through Moses. Let's not forget Jesus' plain statement in John 7:19, "Did not Moses give you the law?" John also records that "the law was given through Moses" (John 1:17). Herbert Armstrong's argument severing Exodus 12 from the law of Moses is misguided and contrived.

Both the food laws and festival laws are, and always have been, part of the law God gave the children of Israel through Moses, the mediator of the Old Covenant. They are, indisputably, part of the law of Moses.

Mr. Armstrong also claims these festival observances occurred "prior to the time when God revealed to Moses and the Israelites He would make the Old Covenant with them." This is an attempt to distance the festivals not only from the law of Moses but also from the Old Covenant. Is this a valid assumption? Are the festivals somehow not part of the Old Covenant? Of course not. The events of Exodus 12-14 have everything to do with God's covenant with Israel and are not separate from it. This is yet another example of an argument that is "not Scriptural."

A study of Exodus will reveal that, from the beginning, God is concerned with his covenant with Abraham, Isaac, Jacob, and the children of Israel. God saw Jacob's children suffering in Egypt and was touched by their plight. "So God heard their groaning, and God *remembered His covenant* with Abraham, with Isaac, and with Jacob. And God looked upon the *children of Israel*, and God acknowledged them" (Ex. 2:24-25).

God again is reminded of his covenant in Exodus 6:4-5, "I have established My covenant with them, to give them the land of Canaan, the land of their pilgrimage, in which they were strangers. And I have also heard the groaning of *the children of Israel* whom the Egyptians keep in bondage, *and I have remembered My covenant.*" Exodus begins with God's intent to enter into a covenant relationship with Israel.

You will recall the beautifully poetic and romantic passage in Ezekiel 16 describing God's covenant relationship with Israel. He tenderly rescues Israel at birth from an untimely death, and lovingly cares for her until she is a beautiful young woman of marriageable age. Notice how God depicts his betrothal to her.

> "'When I passed by you again and looked upon you, indeed your time was the time of love; so I spread My wing over you and covered your nakedness. Yes, I swore an oath to you *and entered into a covenant with you*, and you became mine,' says the Lord God" (Ezek.16:8).

Ezekiel 16 and the Book of Exodus concern God's establishment of a covenant relationship with the children of Israel. The Passover of Exodus 12 was a central event in this covenant story and cannot be disassociated from it. Herbert Armstrong may have sought to prove that the Passover and annual festivals fall outside God's covenant with Israel, but that is not a distinction or separation God makes anywhere in his Word, nor should we. Mr. Armstrong tried to verify that the first Passover occurred "long before" the law of Moses and the Old Covenant were established, but the Bible makes it clear they were contemporaneous events.

The annual festivals or sabbaths are as much a part of the law of Moses as the dietary laws. Most Christian churches have known this all along. No doubt many

Christians who read <u>Pagan Holidays—Or God's Holy Days—Which?</u> over the years rejected Mr. Armstrong's assertions precisely on those grounds.

Like the dietary laws, the annual festivals derive their authority from the law of Moses, and as such, are no longer binding or required of Christians. Attempts to make them so using other "proofs" will be the subject of the next chapter.

Chapter Nine

Categories of Proof

In the preceding chapter we examined Herbert Armstrong's alleged proofs that the annual festivals are not part of the law of Moses. In this chapter I want to broaden that discussion to show how suitable proofs can and should be applied to establish truth and sound doctrine.

There are various legitimate proofs and methods one can choose to examine "evidence." Traditionally in the Worldwide Church of God we relied on certain categories of proofs, often discounting or altogether ignoring others. The unique style of argumentation that permeated our literature appealed to many readers, but I daresay most were unaware of the assumptions underlying our process of reasoning. Unfortunately, certain of these assumptions were faulty and inevitably led to a number of doctrinal positions that were flawed and misleading.

One assumption was that an appeal to law— "*God's* Law"!—was the highest level of proof, and as such, was indisputable. Since we arbitrarily characterized most law appearing in the Bible (minus the sacrifices and ceremonies) as "God's Law," it was viewed as the absolute and final authority. Hence, the church established many of its doctrines and practices by appealing to Old Testament laws as proof. The tithing *laws*, food *laws*, weekly, annual, and even land sabbath *laws* illustrate this point.

By contrast, New Testament statements, particularly in the epistles, and most particularly *Paul's* epistles, carried less weight, and were often labeled "difficult Scriptures" if they compromised or contradicted our doctrinal positions.

So the Worldwide Church of God had a style of proving things and also a hierarchy of proofs. Some kinds of proof were seen as better than others. We also had a certain mix of proofs—certain proportions in which these proofs were blended together to make the case and prove the point.

In reviewing our old literature, I can see clearly that on the subject of the annual sabbaths our mix was heavy on proofs from the law and prophecy and very light on New Testament teaching passages, especially if they were found in the Epistles of Paul.

It is not hard for me to see now in retrospect that our use and weighting of proofs amounted to nothing less than a pro-Old Covenant bias. We weren't, however, the only church that weighted its arguments in this manner. I have come to understand that all sabbatarian groups (including Sunday-keeping sabbatarians, i.e., Christians who believe we should keep a Sunday sabbath) have a similar bias in their style or slant of proof and argumentation. They all reveal a similar bias, depending almost exclusively on Old Covenant, law-based, "legalistic" proofs. And they all seem perplexed by, and are even somewhat suspicious of, the Apostle Paul, whose writings seem to them disturbingly "liberal."

Let's get an overview now of how to use Bible proofs *correctly* to establish doctrine. We will discuss five major types or categories. Understanding them can help us to process the recent changes we've experienced in the Worldwide Church of God. Part of the confusion we have experienced of late stems from the fact that our style of proof is different today from what it has been in the past. Because it doesn't somehow sound the same, it doesn't seem to be as convincing.

Old Testament Laws

First I would like to examine Old Testament laws and commandments. How heavily should these be weighted when used as proof for establishing Christian doctrine and practice?

There are many Old Testament laws; the Jewish rabbis traditionally counted 613. These hundreds of laws governed and regulated diverse matters such as foods, festivals, sexual relations, garments, hygiene and disease, agriculture and animal care, punishments for lawbreaking, and the raising up of seed (i.e., children) to a dead brother.

Which of these should we look to for authority today? All of them? None of them? Some of them? And if some, which ones? And who says?

Does merely quoting an Old Testament law forbidding the wearing of "mixed fabrics" *prove* it should be practiced by Christians today? We used to think so in the Worldwide Church of God! When I came into the church in the late 50's and throughout much of the 60's, wearing clothing made of mixed fabrics was seriously frowned upon and actually *forbidden* in some cases! It was seen as contrary to the Law of God.

What about giving farmland a rest every seven years? We advised a good many farmers to do just that in those early years, and many went bankrupt as a result. But that was in the law, too.

There are three tithes spoken of in the law. How many of those are Christians required to pay? "All three," we said without hesitation, "It's in the Law of God!" And keeping the annual sabbaths or festivals? Same answer, same logic, same proof. If it was in the law, and wasn't clearly ceremonial or sacrificial, Christians—at least Worldwide Church of God Christians—were expected to "just do it."

We all can see the problems and pitfalls associated with this logic. We all know that the New Testament changed and modified many of the Old Testament laws. There were laws requiring both circumcision and sacrifices, but we know those laws are no longer binding under the New Covenant. We know, too, from Hebrews, that the laws of the priesthood were extensively revised when Jesus became our High Priest.

Paul makes clear in Hebrews 8:13 that the Old Covenant is "obsolete"—no longer in effect; therefore, it is invalid to appeal to the Old Covenant legal package as an authority to establish doctrine and practice for New Testament Christians.

The Worldwide Church of God and the Jewish Christians in Acts 15 made a similar mistake. The Jewish Christians, believing the law of Moses was still binding, appealed to that law to prove their case. To them, the law of Moses was the final authority, but Peter made it clear that the law of Moses was not the final proof of doctrine or practice for Christians under the New Covenant. It doubtless came as a shock to those present that the law of Moses was no longer the weightiest proof nor the final authority.

It may still come as a shock and disappointment to some, but a careful study the New Testament will show that this is true. Seldom, if ever, in the New Testament is a matter judged or decided solely on the basis of Old Testament law. I am aware that Jesus effectively used the law in his disputes with the lawyers, scribes and Pharisees (who, it should be noted, were still under the Old Covenant at the time these confrontations occurred), but matters of faith and doctrine in the New Covenant church are not settled that way.

Many view the Ten Commandments as *the* ultimate authority. But no New Testament author, including Jesus Christ, ever uses the term or tries to prove anything solely by an appeal to "the Ten Commandments."

Please understand, I am not opposed to the Ten Commandments or any other Old Testament law or command. I am only trying to put them in their proper perspective as *proofs*. That something was commanded in the Old Testament or under the Old Covenant carries some weight, to be sure. But since that legal code was extensively modified by Jesus Christ himself, beginning with The Sermon on the Mount, we need to be careful about "laying down the law" just because we see something written in the Old Testament.

Old Testament laws and commandments do carry weight as proof, but each must be understood and applied in the light of the New Testament and New Covenant teachings. Failure to do this would, among other things, oblige Christians to wear phylacteries, attach blue fringes to their garments (I remember one church member who argued for that very thing!), wear only clothes made of single fabrics, and to circumcise their baby boys.

New Testament Commands

The next category of proofs for doctrine we will examine is New Testament laws and commands. These are fewer in number and, in the main, less controversial, although not all Christians are entirely agreed on this either, sad to say.

We have, for example, Jesus' "new commandment" to love one another in John 13:34. Baptism is clearly commanded in Acts 2:38. Christ's commission to the Church to preach the Gospel is given in command form in Matthew 28:19-20. And taking of the wine and bread (Christians continue to dispute about what to call this—Communion, Eucharist, "Lord's Supper"; we called it "Passover") is commanded by Jesus with the words, "This *do* in remembrance of me" (I Cor. 11:24).

Few of these New Testament commands have Old Testament precedents, but they are still seen as weighty and powerful proofs and are deemed by Christians as the final authority. In the Sermon on the Mount Jesus actually rescinded certain Old Testament laws with new commandments of his own. His statement on oaths is a good example:

> "Again you have heard that it was said to those of old, 'You shall not swear falsely, but shall perform your oaths to the Lord.' But I say to you, do not swear at all: neither by heaven, for it is God's throne; nor by earth, for it is his footstool; nor by Jerusalem, for it is the city of the great King" (Matt. 5:33-34).

Again, the Sermon on the Mount illustrates how Old Testament commandments are modified by New Testament commands. Clearly, where there is conflict, New Testament commands take precedence over Old Testament commandments and therefore constitute a higher authority.

Prophecy

Next, we will examine prophecy as a category of proof. Prophecy has often been cited, along with Old Testament laws, as proof for the observance of the annual festivals.

Zechariah 14 is perhaps the best known example of prophetic proof for the annual festivals. There we find that "all nations...shall go up from year to year to worship the King, and to keep the Feast of Tabernacles" (Zech 14:16). This is one prophecy about the annual sabbaths. Another predicts the observance of the sabbath and new moons during the millennial reign of Christ on earth:

> "For as the new heavens and the new earth which I will make shall remain before me," says the Lord, "So shall your descendants and your name remain. And it shall come to pass that from one New Moon to another, and from one Sabbath to another, all flesh shall come to worship before Me," says the Lord (Isa. 66:22-23).

Putting together these two prophetic passages, we have incontrovertible proof that all Christians today should be keeping the sabbath, new moons, and annual festivals, right? Because things that God will require of people in the future are surely required of us today, aren't they? That's often been a line of reasoning used in the Worldwide Church of God to prove festival observance.

Then how shall we understand the prophecy of Zechariah 13:2-3? It says:

> "It shall be in that day," says the Lord of hosts, "that I will cut off the names of the idols from the land...I will also cause the

prophets and the unclean spirit to depart from the land. It shall come to pass that if anyone still prophesies, then his father and his mother who begot him will say to him, 'You shall not live, because you have spoken lies in the name of the Lord.' And his father and mother who begot him shall thrust him through when he prophesies."

Clearly, false prophets will be put to death in Christ's kingdom. If prophecy proves what Christians today should do, then we should also put to death false prophets, according to that line of reasoning. And what about the prophecies of Ezekiel 40-48 which, if they are to be taken literally, indicate the reinstitution of the priesthood, sin offerings, and the Temple?

It should be obvious from these examples that prophecies for the future cannot be seen as reliable guides to determine what Christians should be doing now. If they were, we should all be keeping new moons, offering up sin offerings in a Temple, and putting false prophets to death. Prophecies concerning the future, whether for the millennium or World Tomorrow, as we've called it in the Worldwide Church of God, or the time of the New Heavens and New Earth, are prophecies for those future times and cannot be used as authoritative proofs for Christian doctrine and practice today.

While it may be true that all nations after Christ's return will go up to Jerusalem to keep the Feast of Tabernacles, we read of no such practice in the New Testament. The observance of the Feast of Tabernacles is nowhere mentioned as a practice of the New Testament Church, nor is there any record of Christians keeping it at Jerusalem or anywhere else.

The Feast of Tabernacles is prophesied to be a major event for Israel, Egypt, and all nations in the coming Kingdom era. It does *not* seem to have been a major event for New Testament Christians. No one ever commands its observance, records its observance, or explains its meaning for Christians today. In the Worldwide Church of God over the years, we often claimed that God's plan of salvation cannot be understood apart from the weekly and annual sabbaths, but we find nothing in the Bible to back this claim. It would seem many new Christians, such as the Philippian jailer of Acts 16, came to repentance and baptism with little or no understanding of the meaning of the annual festivals.

So what kind of proof is prophecy? Well, prophecies for and about the present Christian era, such as those Peter expounded on Pentecost concerning the death, burial and resurrection of Christ (see Acts 2:27-31) of course carry great weight and authority for our time today. And prophecies for the future carry similar weight and authority for the future, but we shouldn't confuse the two.

Prophetic proofs must be carefully used and properly understood. We need to understand that something prophesied for the future does not prove it is binding on and required of us as Christians today.

Bible Examples

Let us look next at Bible examples as a category of proof. These, too, are often used to "prove" the annual sabbaths. In the Bible we read that Jesus kept the Passover with his family as a youth (Luke 2:41-42), and later as an adult he went up to Jerusalem to keep the Feast of Tabernacles (John 7:10). So that conclusively proves we should do the same, doesn't it?

The apostles in Acts and the epistles are found observing, or at least noting, the festivals of Passover, the Days of Unleavened Bread, and Pentecost. Shouldn't we do all the things that Jesus and the apostles did and follow their example? Isn't what they did clear proof of what we should be doing today?

That line of reasoning is plausible and attractive, but it is also simplistic and misleading. For example, we know from the Bible that Jesus was, as a baby boy, circumcised on the eighth day (Luke 2:21) as was the apostle Paul (Phil. 3:5). Should Christians follow their example and circumcise their male children today? And should all males be circumcised when they become Christians?

No, we know that isn't true. Why not? Because we have Christian doctrine and teaching to the contrary. We have passages of Scripture in the New Testament showing that circumcision is no longer binding or required for Christians' children or newly converted adults. This illustrates that biblical example of and by itself isn't the highest form of proof. Example must be understood in the light of New Testament teaching.

Paul's personal example was to remain single and unmarried (I Cor. 7). But his example does not make celibacy binding and required for all Christians. Paul is careful to explain that some things are by commandment and others are by permission (allowable choice). Paul was at liberty to remain single. He could even recommend it for others (I Cor.7:7), but he could not command anyone to remain unmarried. His personal example did not constitute church policy. This is an important distinction, and one that we have not always been clear about in the Worldwide Church of God.

Like proofs from Old Testament law and prophecy, Bible examples must be properly understood and carefully qualified. We do indeed have the example of Christ, the apostles, and many in the New Testament church observing the annual festivals, but we need to ask whether they did so by permission or commandment. Did Christ and the apostles consider the annual festivals a binding requirement for all Christians? Or were they rather something that was permitted and approved but not done "by commandment"?

We read in Acts 18:21 that Paul told the brethren at Ephesus, "I must by all means keep this coming feast in Jerusalem." Can this verse be used to prove that all Christians should do the same? Is Paul instructing the church about festival observance or merely giving them his personal travel plans? There is nothing here or elsewhere to suggest that Paul expected all Christians to follow him to Jerusalem to keep the upcoming feast.

As we have seen, simply because we find an example of someone doing something in the Bible is not in and of itself proof positive it is binding and required of everyone, or else all Christian males, following the example of Jesus and Paul, would be circumcised and celibate!

New Testament Teaching

Finally, let's look now at New Testament teaching as another type of proof and authority. As noted above, there are laws requiring circumcision and sacrifices, but as Christians today we do not believe we are obliged to keep those laws. Why not? Because we have New Testament teaching and instruction to the contrary. There are prophecies for the future that we do not view as binding in their authority for us today. Why not? Again, because of New Testament teaching.

This acquaints us with the weight and authority of New Testament teaching and instructional passages. They operate on a higher level of authority than either Old Testament law or prophecy and, along with New Testament commands, are the supreme authority to which Christians should look when determining doctrine and practice in the church today.

We understand how New Testament teaching modifies Old Testament laws and prophecy on matters such as circumcision, sacrifices, and the priesthood. But do we also accept its authority on such matters as meats and sabbath days? Or do we make the mistake of weighting law and prophecy over plain New Testament instruction? I'm afraid that is exactly what we did in years past in the Worldwide Church of God, following our own notions of what constitutes "proof."

There is New Testament teaching on the annual festivals just as there is on foods and meats. There are verses that speak directly to the matter of "a festival, or a new moon or sabbaths." There are several passages in which the observance of such days is discussed and explained. Have we let these authoritative passages shape our doctrine and practice, or have we largely dismissed them as "difficult scriptures" in the hard-to-be-understood Epistles of Paul?

Speaking from my own experience, I would have to say we looked at such passages with deep suspicion and distrust if not downright hostility. We did not refer to these New Testament instructional passages much at all. Rather, law, prophecy, and Bible example were seen as more authoritative proofs than plain New Testament teaching. Why? Because these passages did not fit our prevailing Old Covenant doctrinal paradigm. Our solution was to produce imaginative explanations that usually reversed the originally intended meaning of the verses. It is clear to me now that we simply could not accept what the many New Testament teaching passages . on the annual festivals had to say. Instead, we had to radically revise and reinterpret them to fit our doctrinal scheme.

Thankfully, as the result of the reforms we have experienced of late, we have come out of this doctrinal denial and can now openly examine what these passages actually say. We will do just that in the next chapter, but let's first briefly review this discussion of categories of proofs.

We've looked at five categories of proofs: Old Testament laws, New Testament laws, prophecy, Bible example and New Testament teaching and instruction. We've seen that it is New Testament commands and teaching that are the strongest proofs and carry the highest level of authority for Christians today. We have noted that Old Testament law, prophecy, and even the example of Jesus and the apostles must be interpreted and understood in the light of New Testament teaching and commands.

If, for example, both Old Testament laws and Bible prophecy seem to suggest the observance of new moons (and they do), and New Testament teaching suggests that their observance is not required (and it does), then Christians abide by the New Testament teaching and do not require the observance of new moons.

Traditionally, following the lead of Herbert Armstrong, we have not always done this. On important doctrinal issues, including the dietary laws and annual festivals, we have weighted Old Testament laws, prophecy, and

Bible examples over New Testament instructions and commands. The way we went about determining or "proving" our doctrines was very convincing to many, but it brought us to various wrong conclusions.

It is time to correct not only these wrong doctrinal conclusions but also the methods that produced them. It is time to bring both in line with the teaching of the New Covenant of Jesus Christ, not the Old Covenant and the law of Moses.

We will now give our full attention to the New Testament instructional passages on the annual festivals.

Chapter Ten

The Verse Herbert Armstrong Couldn't Explain

In the New Testament, God has given us several authoritative passages that comment specifically on the observance of days, including the weekly and annual sabbaths and the new moons. Although they comprise God's New Covenant instructions, and are regarded by most Christians as authoritative statements on the subject, these scriptures, unfortunately, were dismissed and devalued by the Worldwide Church of God.

In reviewing our traditional explanations of these passages, it became apparent to me that various techniques were used to minimize their importance. First, they were dismissed out-of-hand as though they didn't require further explanation. Second, they were labeled "difficult scriptures" because we had great difficulty explaining them according to our doctrinal world view. Third, when we did try to explain these passages, we invariably had to concoct odd and strange interpretations which seemed to undermine the context of the passage as well as the author's original intent.

The net result was a patchwork quilt of explanations. All of the verses in question are actually quite similar in content and intent, yet we assigned a different interpretation to each. Where one would expect a certain unity and coherence, one found instead a hodgepodge of ideas all pointing in different directions, with no common threads or unifying themes.

One striking feature in the literature we published on this subject is that over the years we explained these verses different ways at different times. In this chapter we will examine these contradictory interpretations, and show how elusive the "plain truth" can be when one labors, as we did, under an erroneous premise.

Let's begin with the verse that Herbert Armstrong could not—or would not—explain. I think you will find this eye-opening. I know I did.

A correct understanding of Colossians 2:16 is critically important to the question, "What days are Christians required to observe?" In Romans and Galatians the exact nature of the days under discussion is arguable. Some say, as the Worldwide Church of God once did, that the days Paul admonishes Galatians about in Galatians 4:10 are pagan, Gentile holidays. Sabbatarians usually interpret the days mentioned in Romans 14 as fast days of some kind, not days for worship. (We will examine these passages and positions later.)

In Colossians 2:16, however, we have a verse that unquestionably refers to the sabbaths and new moons of the Old Testament, "Therefore let no one judge you in food or drink, or regarding a festival or a new moon or sabbaths." There can be no confusion regarding the meaning of "a festival or a new moon or sabbaths." Sabbaths were clearly not of Gentile or pagan origin.

In Colossians 2:16 we have the most critically important verse of the New Testament regarding the observance or non-observance of the days enjoined as statutes under the law of Moses. Of all the passages in the New Testament on the subject, this verse strikes right to the heart of the sacred days dispute. It is essential that we get this one right.

So how did Herbert Armstrong explain this verse? Well, actually *he didn't*. We will shortly see how he dismissed it without any real explanation. Most uncharacteristically, he left the task of explaining this verse to others.

Herbert Armstrong's treatment of Colossians 2:16 can be found in his <u>Pagan Holidays—or God's Holy Days—Which?</u> It appears in the same introductory passage I quoted from earlier in connection with the law of Moses. Let's examine a few paragraphs to see how he presents his case. Under the subhead "Study This Twice," Mr. Armstrong writes:

> Let us warn, too, that certain objections will be sure to come to mind—all of which, will be dealt with and explained later on.... Such arguments as 'The annual Sabbaths are part of the law of Moses,' ...or 'Col.2:16 does away with the annual Sabbaths,' are not Scriptural.[1]

Here Mr. Armstrong states two of the most serious objections to the observance of the annual festivals—namely, that they are part of the law of Moses (which we have already carefully examined), and the problem posed by Colossians 2:16, which labels these days as "shadows." Yet he devotes only one paragraph to Colossians 2:16 in which he repeats his earlier argument that "the weekly Sabbath and annual Sabbaths stand or fall together":

> Colossians 2:16 refers, not ALONE to the annual sabbaths, but to the annual days, the monthly new moons, AND the weekly SABBATH. Whenever the Bible uses the expression "sabbath days" with new moons and holy days, it is referring to THE WEEKLY SABBATH DAYS, the ANNUAL holy days or feast days...If Colossians does away with the one, it also abolishes the other.[2]

The argument is simple and direct, but it explains nothing. He says, in effect, that Colossians 2:16 treats both the weekly and annual sabbaths the same way, and since "we all know the weekly sabbath is binding, we know Colossians 2:16 can't possibly be used against the observance of the annual sabbaths or festivals." That is Mr. Armstrong's *entire* "explanation" of the verse!

But what is meant by "let no man judge you"? Why did Paul call sabbaths and new moons "a shadow of things to come" in verse 17? What did Paul mean by "shadow"? And following Mr. Armstrong's line of reasoning that all of the things spoken of in this verse stand or fall together, shouldn't Christians, then, also observe the new moons?

Herbert Armstrong is, on any and all of these matters, strangely silent. He, perhaps very wisely, does not try to explain this verse. I can find no place in the Worldwide Church of God literature index where he ever tried. He merely dismisses it by declaring that since it obviously can't be used against the weekly sabbath, it can't be used against the annual sabbaths either. He makes no other attempt to explain the meaning of this *critically important* verse.

What about this approach? Is it responsible? For years, we in the church simply went along with this high-handed, authoritarian style of scriptural exegesis. It is astonishing that a verse as important as Colossians 2:16 could be so casually dismissed, and that efforts to bring it into the discussion were branded "not Scriptural."

What about God's admonition that we "search the Scriptures" and "prove all things"? If we truly believe "all Scripture is given by inspiration of God, and is profitable for doctrine," then we must apply that principle to the study of Colossians 2:16.

The church's casual treatment of Colossians 2:16 did not result in a right and proper understanding of this important verse. Once again, we must critically evaluate not only the conclusions but also the methods we used to support our views—for here is yet another example of how we were led off track.

Later Attempts at Explaining Colossians 2:16

In the later literature of the Worldwide Church of God, there were two separate attempts to explain Colossians 2:16, neither of which was written by Herbert Armstrong. Both appeared in The Good News, a magazine offered to church members and co-workers. The first of these appeared in the September, 1960 issue under the title, Does It Matter What Days We Observe? The second, The Colossian Heresy, appeared in the July/August, 1989 issue, more than three years after Herbert Armstrong's death. The articles were written by different authors and have substantial differences between them.

Let me briefly summarize how each article treats Colossians 2:16-17. The 1960 Good News article concludes that the Christians at Colossae were being judged by the ascetic Gentile community for their observance of the sabbaths, new moons, and festivals. According to the author, "They were enjoying the Christian life in temperance and self-control, and especially in connection with each feast, every new moon and the weekly sabbaths!"

Then what did Paul mean by his statement that these days were "shadows of things to come"? Doesn't that suggest that once the reality of these days had been fulfilled in Christ, their observance was no longer required? No, not according to this article. "Shadow" acquires a curiously positive quality, and the author arbitrarily declares that it is "better translated 'which foreshadow things to come.'" Precisely why that is a better translation is not explained.

But based on that interpretation, the author develops his explanation of "shadow":

> Did these scriptural days foreshadow things to come? Indeed! Does the weekly sabbath foreshadow things to come? Indeed!...
> In like manner the annual festivals, instituted as *memorials*, also foreshadow the plan of God. They were given to the Church in order to keep the Church in the knowledge of that plan.[4]

So the phrase "shadows of things to come" is viewed auspiciously, and is not to be contrasted, in the usual literary sense, with either substance or reality. According to this view, shadows are actually *fore*shadows of the plan of God, and as such, Christians must continue to observe them.

That is, at the very least, an original interpretation; the word shadow is never used in the scriptures to mean the foreshadowing of yet future events.

In this same article we find yet another explanation seldom found outside the Worldwide Church of God. The article goes on to define "the body of Christ" (v.17), not as the contrasting term for shadow, but as a reference to the church of God, citing Colossians 1:18 as proof, "And He is the head of the body, the church..."

According to this argument, we should let no one judge us concerning our observance of sabbaths, new moons, and festivals, *except* the church of God. Thus, the church had the power and authority to determine whether the annual festivals should be kept, and appropriating that authority, the Worldwide Church of God determined, of course, that they *should.*

This innovative, prophetic interpretation of "shadows" coupled with equating the body of Christ with the church was, for years, the backbone of the church's teaching on Colossians 2:16-17. Countless "difficult scripture sermonettes" were given at Ambassador College and in local congregations, rehearsing these ideas, and following this line of reasoning.

The 1989 Good News piece on Colossians, however, took a different tack altogether. This article argues for the unconditional adequacy of Christ and that Christians are complete in him. The author, for the first time in Worldwide Church of God literature, allows that Paul indeed is contrasting shadow with body or substance. Thus, he departs from the earlier "foreshadow" interpretation and does not try to make "body of Christ" into the church of God:

> The matters listed, despite the claims
> of the Colossian heretics, could not transcend
> Christ, who is now the *body* (emphasis his),
> the substance, the very center of God's plan
> of salvation. All else is a mere *shadow* that
> holds no value as a replacement for Christ.[5]

This article was published more than three years after Herbert Armstrong's death. It is doubtful, in my opinion, that it could have been written and published during his lifetime. For the first time in our church literature, "shadow" and "body" were contrasted in the typical way in which the verse is translated and understood. More to the point, *shadow is used the way the Bible elsewhere uses the term.* "Shadow" no longer is used to convey

115

an attractive meaning or a "foreshadowing" of yet future events. The article continues,

> The heretics, then, were ignorantly trying to push the church of Colossae out of the light and into shadows. Even God's law had a "shadow of good things to come." Even so, it could not "make the comers thereunto perfect" (Hebrews 10:1).[6]

And in this same article we see, *again for the first time*, another Bible passage introduced in which the term shadow appears. Hebrews 10 uses that same term when discussing the sacrificial law. Perhaps we can see why Mr. Armstrong was not inclined to delve into the verse, its words, and its meaning. He may not have wished to see the sabbaths and new moons associated with the now unnecessary animal sacrifices.

The 1989 explanation of Colossians 2:16-17 headed in the right direction and moved closer to the full meaning of the passage. The author rightly prioritizes Christ over commandment keeping. He writes,

> Paul is not saying that there is no value to obeying God's law. He is saying that any act one could care to mention—circumcision, keeping new moons, sabbaths, etc. (2:11-17)—cannot replace or transcend Christ...
>
> Paul could point out that, without Christ at the center, absolutely nothing would stand, no matter how many of God's commandments one would care to keep, and no matter how strictly one were to keep them.[7]

As much as it was a step forward, the article left unanswered whether the sabbaths and new moons are required of Christians today. It courageously addressed words and related verses that Herbert Armstrong so carefully avoided, but failed to arrive at any practical conclusions. To be fair, given where the Worldwide Church of God stood on doctrinal matters in June 1989, only three and a half years after Mr. Armstrong's death, that is all it could be expected to do.

Did we all "speak the same thing" over the years? Hardly. On this verse, for which understanding about observances is so critical, we have had different arguments and explanations at different times by different ministers and authors.

We need to be mature and honest enough to acknowledge this very imperfect state of affairs. Can we humbly admit to having had a poor understanding, at best, of the one verse on sacred days we should understand the most, and the one for which we should have a good, clear, and consistent explanation?

I would like now to examine this verse even more fully in its New Testament context and squarely face its implications. It is time—in fact, long past time—that we do.

Chapter Eleven

Colossians 2:16-17
as the Bible Explains It

Colossians 2:16-17 is not at all difficult to understand if we follow a principle we often quoted in the Worldwide Church of God. We always said we should let the Bible interpret the Bible. We said we should let the Bible explain itself. And we always said we could understand a Bible subject by putting together all the Scriptures that pertain to that subject.

What I am about to show you is that *all* the key terms and phrases used in Colossians 2:16-17 can be found in other New Testament passages. Two of the phrases essential to understanding this scripture are found elsewhere in Paul's writings. Both shed considerable light on what Paul meant to convey.

In the previous chapters we saw how the Worldwide Church of God formerly explained these verses and how it was not until after Herbert Armstrong's death that church scholars were able to discuss in writing the "difficult scripture" passages found in Paul's epistles. In this chapter we will come to understand these verses just as Paul meant them to be understood. But I must tell you in advance that when you understand what Paul really meant, you no longer will be able to accept the Worldwide Church of God's traditional explanation of Colossians 2:16-17.

The beauty of Colossians 2:16 is that, in one verse, we have all of the days that were observed in the Old Testament laid out before us—the festivals, new moons, and sabbaths. There is *no doubt* which days are under discussion. They cannot be confused with either pagan days or fast days. The identity of the days in Colossians 2:16 is perfectly clear.

In verse 17, we have God's New Testament teaching on these days. The writer is, of course, the Apostle Paul, and virtually all Christians believe he was writing under divine inspiration. So this is not Paul's commentary on these days, but *God's* commentary through Paul.

Verse 17 says that these days "are a shadow of things to come, but the substance is of Christ" (NKJV). I am keenly aware of the controversy surrounding the last phrase, and whether it should be translated body, substance, reality, etc., and I will deal with that matter later on. But for now, let's begin with the word "shadow."

Shadow Means Shadow

When Paul said that the days of the Old Covenant were shadows, he *meant* that they were shadows. You see, we have been so conditioned in the Worldwide Church of God over the years to deny the obvious intent of these verses that it takes quite an effort to go back to a logical starting point. Some will find it hard to focus their minds on the main thrust of Paul's argument because of the church's prior teaching on this subject. But to capture what Paul is trying to say, we need to start with a discussion about shadows.

A proper understanding of Col.2:16 hinges on Paul's use of the term "shadow" in verse 17. Paul is, of course, using a common literary device—the metaphor.

When he calls all the days of the Old Covenant "a shadow," shadow becomes Paul's *metaphor* for the sabbaths, new moons, and festivals.

Let's see how the shadow metaphor is commonly used in literature in general and how it is used by Paul and other Bible writers in particular.

As a metaphor, shadow is typically used in contrast with either light or substance. When contrasted with light, a shadow pictures something dark, hidden, obscure, vague or unclear. For example, an author might write that "a shadowy figure lurked at the foot of the tenement stairs." The author intends the reader to envision a discernible human form, but whose identity is obscured by the surrounding darkness.

When contrasted with substance, shadow suggests that which is fleeting, changing, temporary, or impermanent, as in Psalm 109:23, "I am gone like a shadow when it lengthens." Here, David likens his existence to a shadow that grows longer and longer as the day declines, until at sunset, it disappears and is gone. Shadow is the beautiful and poetic image David chose to depict the fleeting, impermanent nature of life.

Let's look at some additional Bible uses of the term. We find shadow contrasted with light in Luke 1:79, referring to John the Baptist. He was "to give light to those who sit in darkness and the shadow of death."

Jesus' public ministry was announced using similar wording, "The people who sat in darkness saw a great light, And upon those who sat in the region of shadow of death Light has dawned" (Matt. 4:16).

Bible students will also be familiar with the use of shadow in a verse that describes God the Father. We read in James 1:17 that "every good gift and every perfect gift is from above, and comes down from the Father of lights, with whom there is no variation or shadow of turning" (NKJV).

Here, shadow is contrasted with light, but it also suggests something moveable and impermanent. Notice how the same verse is translated in the <u>New International Version</u>, "Every good and perfect gift is from...the Father of the heavenly lights, who does not change like shifting shadows."

Moving objects cast shifting, changing shadows, but God is not "shadowy" in any respect. Full of light, he is steady, real, and permanent.

When it is used as a metaphor (as in the above verse—"like shifting shadows"), shadow usually is not cast in a favorable light. When we say someone is "a shadowy character," we do not mean it as a compliment. The one exception to this in the Bible is the term "shadow of his wings" in the Psalms and elsewhere, denoting divine protection. All other uses have negative connotations. Fleeting, temporary human life, for example, is often described as "passing like a shadow" (Eccl. 6:12, 8:13).

Now that we've looked at examples of the general, literary use of shadow in the Bible and elsewhere, let's see how Paul specifically uses the term. Hebrews 10:1 is the most illustrative passage, and we will examine it first:

"For the law, having a shadow of the
good things to come, and not the very image
of the things, can never with these same
sacrifices, which they offer continually year
by year, make those who approach perfect."

Let me explain that I am here and throughout leaning toward the traditional notion that Paul, though unnamed in the book, is the author of Hebrews. I am aware of the many good reasons that some have for thinking he is not, but my personal feeling is that Paul is the only New Testament writer with the spiritual and intellectual capacity to write Hebrews. (If you are interested, you can find a good discussion of the pro's and con's of Paul's authorship of Hebrews in Donald Guthrie's <u>Introduction to the New Testament</u>.)[1]   But my argument doesn't rest entirely on Paul's being the author. If it was not Paul, then some other New Testament writer, inspired by God's Spirit, is shedding light on the word shadow as it is used in the Bible.

In any case, here in Hebrews 10 we find Paul—or some other New Testament person like Luke, Timothy, Apollos, Barnabas, Silvanus, or Priscilla (and each of them has been suggested)—using language that is almost identical to the language used in Colossians 2. It is "a shadow of things to come" in Colossians, and "a shadow of the good things to come" in Hebrews.

Surely we would all agree that the use of such a similar phrase by the same author—or a contemporaneous author—in one context can be used to shed light on what that author means in another context. Indeed, the author of Hebrews uses the terms shadow and things to come, not once, but twice in Hebrews. Examining both passages should make very clear what he meant.

The first thing that I would call to your attention is that when using the phrase in Hebrews, Paul (back to my preferred author for Hebrews, once again, and so hereafter) contrasts shadow with "image." The Greek word here is the word from which we derive our English word icon. A shadow can give a shape or an outline, but not the whole picture or image. So the use of the term shadow in Hebrews is contrasted with image or likeness. Some versions like the NIV prefer "realities," which is a less literal translation but one that captures well the thought.

A few chapters earlier in Hebrews, Paul uses shadow to signify a copy or pattern. Speaking of Jesus as our High Priest, he writes,

> "For if he were on earth, He would not be a priest, since there are priests who offer gifts according to the law; who serve the copy and shadow of the heavenly things, as Moses was divinely instructed when he was about to make the tabernacle. For He said, 'See that you make all things according to the pattern shown you on the mountain'" (Heb. 8:4-5).

So in these verses, the shadow, copy, or pattern of the tabernacle is contrasted with "the true tabernacle" mentioned in verse 2. As I've shown, shadow is a term often used in contrast to something else. This point of fact will help us to understand the meaning of Colossians 2:16-17.

Now let's see what Paul's use of shadow in Hebrews can add to our understanding of Colossians. In Col. 2:17, he makes a similar contrast: "body" ("soma" in Greek) is contrasted with shadow. Body and shadow are also commonly contrasted images. You could see someone's approaching shadow, perhaps on a wall or window shade, or you could also see the same person *bodily*, "in the flesh," as we say. The shadow might leave some doubt about the person's identity, but seeing them bodily would not. If you saw the body, you wouldn't need the shadow to know who the person was.

For Paul, the various days of the Old Covenant cast shadowy outlines of things—"*good* things"—to come. But the deeper meaning and reality of days such as the Passover and Day of Atonement, both of which Paul explains in his epistles, are found in Christ. The use of "substance" or "reality" in most modern translations befits the context and is a most suitable rendering.

To force the *church* to fit into this context compromises the meaning of the passage, as the Broadman Bible Commentary explains:

> To understand *substance* (body) as the church, or the glorified body of Christ, misses the emphasis of the paragraph, well summarized in the NEB, 'the solid reality is Christ's' (cf. Heb. 8:5; 10:1 ff).[2]

The earlier Worldwide Church of God interpretation of this verse made this error and truly missed Paul's point. Paul's contrast of shadow and body in Colossians means the same thing as his contrast of shadow and image in Hebrews. Accepting this consistency of language and thought is much preferred, I hope you will agree, over suddenly and unexpectedly introducing into the context the idea of the church. Shadow has a clear, logical, contrasting relationship to image and body that it simply does not have to church.

The NIV translates these verses similarly:

"These are a shadow of the things that were to come, the reality, however is found in Christ" (Col. 2:17).

"The law is only a shadow of the good things that are coming—not the realities themselves" (Heb. 10:1).

These similar translations reflect the consistency of Paul's thought and intent and nicely capture what he meant to say through these metaphors.

But we do not have to let our understanding of Paul's meaning rest on his use of language alone. We can and should also be guided by both the content and the context of these passages in Colossians and Hebrews. Let's shift our attention away from "shadow" now and focus it on "things to come."

What Were "The Good Things to Come"?

We have seen how Paul used the term shadow, but what does he mean by "good things to come"? Paul himself reveals how he meant this to be interpreted through his use of the phrase elsewhere in his writings. But first let us see how that phrase was traditionally understood in the Worldwide Church of God. Under Mr. Armstrong, the value of the festivals and annual holy days, and the most powerful argument for their observance was always that they revealed future events in what we called "the plan of God," or "God's plan of salvation."

I have before me a booklet entitled "What Is Your Destiny?" published by the United Church of God (followers of Herbert Armstrong's teachings who left the Worldwide Church of God to form their own church in response to recent doctrinal changes). Chapter 3, entitled, "God's Master Plan for Mankind's Salvation," continues in the Armstrong tradition of promoting the annual festivals as the way to understand the plan of salvation:

> We have seen that God will reconcile humanity to Himself, "bringing many sons to glory" (Hebrews 2:10). Now we will see that is working according to a master plan symbolized by His annual festivals.
>
> These festivals, listed in Leviticus 23, give us a view of the plan for mankind He is working out here on earth, with each festival revealing a major facet of that plan. God commands us to observe these festivals so we may better understand His master plan of salvation (Psalm 111:10).[3]

Note that the author(s) cite Leviticus 23 for the authority to mandate festival observance and to support their assumption that Christians today must keep these days according to God's command. The booklet fails to address whether the festivals in Leviticus might be part of the law of Moses and therefore not required of Christians. The booklet explains the various festivals in their chronological order and, where deemed appropriate, their prophetic interpretation is given. The Feast of Tabernacles, for example, is seen as picturing the millennial reign of Christ.

So, "shadows of things to come" in our former tradition is always taken to mean that the annual festivals have a prophetic meaning *yet to be fulfilled*. Persons holding this view understandably resist the idea that such meaning-filled days were only shadows that were fulfilled in the substance of Christ and that their observance is no longer mandatory.

In the Worldwide Church of God prior to 1995 (and in its derivative groups still) these festivals were permanent institutions, filled with much future, prophetic importance. After all, isn't that what Paul meant when he said they were "shadows of things *to come*"?

I can understand this position, having believed it myself for years, but, no, that is not at all what Paul meant. For Paul, "the good things to come" *had already arrived* with the coming of Christ, and those days, which anticipated the Messiah, he comfortably described as shadows.

Paul understood the prophetic indications of the annual Old Covenant festivals, but it is quite clear from his writings that he was convinced they had been fulfilled in Christ. When Paul writes of "the good things to come," he always speaks of them as having *already* arrived. They are, for Paul, *historic* events, not *prophesied* events.

127

Good Things to Come

Let's notice now how Paul treats the phrase "good things to come." In Hebrews 9:11, he writes, "But Christ came as High Priest of the good things to come."

Carefully note the wording and the verb tenses used. "Christ *came*"—past tense, historic, accomplished fact—"as the High Priest of good things *to come*." Take time to study how Paul develops the thought of Christ as our "High Priest of the good things to come" in Hebrews 9:11-15. The "good things to come" refer to "His own blood" and "eternal redemption" in 9:12, the purging of the conscience in 9:14, and Christ as the Mediator of the new covenant in 9:15—all exceedingly "good things," which were once prophesied "to come," but are now fully available to us through Christ. Again, for Paul, the meaning of the festivals that were once prophetic had become historic.

Paul's treatment of the Passover found in I Corinthians 5:7 is from the same perspective. "For indeed Christ, our Passover, was sacrificed for us." Notice again, "*was* sacrificed," past tense, not *is* sacrificed. His emphasis is not on the Corinthians' local observance of the festival, but on the accomplished fact of Christ's death and how each member should respond to it. Christ died for the Corinthians, but they as a church were slow to remove sin from their lives. They openly tolerated the fornicator in their midst and somehow even gloried in that fact (verses 1-5).

Paul reminded them that they were now unleavened, not in a limited and literal sense, but spiritually cleansed through Christ's sacrifice, and he urged them to live "unleavened" lives. When they kept the feast it was to be in a new way—"not with old leaven," as some from Jewish backgrounds may have done in the past—but with a deeper appreciation for what those symbols meant and how they had been fulfilled.

Let's look now at the other passage in which Paul refers to "the good things to come." Speaking of the sacrificial law, he writes,

> "For the law, having a shadow of the good things to come, and not the very image of the things, can never with these same sacrifices, which they offer continually year by year, make those who approach perfect"(Heb. 10:1).

The good things anticipated by the sacrifices and offerings were also fulfilled in Christ. They are here, available to us now, in the person of Christ. We no longer need the anticipatory shadows of the sacrifices now that their very image has arrived. And remember, this is *the very same language* Paul uses to describe the sabbaths, new moons, and festivals—"a shadow of things to come."

When expounding the meaning of the Day of Atonement in Hebrews 9, Paul speaks of its historic fulfillment, not of a yet-to-come prophetic realization. Herbert Armstrong's interpretation of Atonement always stressed that Satan fulfilled the role of the symbolic Azazel goat of Leviticus 23, and that he will be bound and later cast out after Christ's return. That may be true, but unlike Mr. Armstrong, Paul did not look at the Day of Atonement prophetically.

Speaking of the Atonement rituals in the Tabernacle, Paul writes,

> "But into the second part the high priest went along once a year, not without blood, which he offered for himself and for

the people's sins committed in ignorance;
the Holy Spirit indicating this, that the
way into the Holiest of All was not yet
made manifest while the first tabernacle
was still standing. It was *symbolic for
the present time* in which both gifts and
sacrifices are offered..." (Heb. 9:7-9).

Paul applies the original symbolism of the Day
of Atonement to what time? To the distant future
after Christ's return? No, only to "the *present* time"!
Under the Old Covenant, the high priest could only
enter into the Holy of Holies once a year to make an
atonement for the sins of the people. After Christ came
and established the New Covenant, we, through him
as our high Priest, have access to God—*continually*. This consistent interpretation of "things to come"
as having *already* arrived is important to note and
to think about.

For Paul, the meaning of Atonement was thus
fulfilled. The day had been a shadow of things to come
which had now arrived through Christ.

Can we begin to see why Paul was comfortable
calling the sabbaths, new moons, and festivals "shadows"—
shadows of things to come that had now come to pass
and had their true substance and meaning fulfilled in
Christ? Unlike Herbert Armstrong, Paul was not
trying to show that all of those Old Covenant/law of
Moses days had some yet-to-be fulfilled, meaning and
significance. Shadow was Paul's metaphor for the Old
Covenant days because he saw them—just as he saw
the sacrificial law—as prefiguring acts and events now
perfectly fulfilled in Christ.

Notice the Expositor's Bible Commentary on Colossians 2:17:

> "All such legal stipulations were but 'a shadow (i.e., an anticipation) of the things that were to come.' Therefore to cling to the prophetic shadow is to obscure the spiritual reality of which those things were a prefigurement. 'The reality' (substance) belongs to Christ. In him, the things to come have come."[4]

That is *exactly* what Paul was saying—"the things to come have come." And the things that anticipated them and prefigured them, whether they were days or sacrifices (and he used this same term for both) are temporary shadows. We no longer need to cling to the shadows or celebrate the shadows. Neither must we staunchly defend the shadows as essential to understanding God's plan of salvation. Nor can we require of others that they celebrate and observe the shadows as something essential for their salvation.

We, as members or former members of the Worldwide Church of God, would have little or no trouble seeing this if we hadn't been so heavily programmed to believe otherwise. I have on several occasions even heard some ministers insist that you cannot understand the plan of salvation *at all* without the holy days. I am quite certain that such a thought would never have occurred to Paul.

Just what about the plan of salvation could one not understand without the festivals of the Old Testament? Christ's life, death, and resurrection? Must we observe days to understand that?

Seeking to put sin out of our lives by the power of Christ in us through the Holy Spirit? Is that incomprehensible to Christians without certain days?

We have always said in the Worldwide Church of God that the Feast of Trumpets pictures Christ's Second Coming at the last trump, and indeed it may. But with entire, clear-cut chapters such as Matthew 24, I Corinthians 15, and II Thessalonians 2, and the powerful apocalyptic language of the Book of Revelation, can we honestly believe that it is impossible to understand the Second Coming of Christ and its role in God's plan, without keeping an Old Testament festival?

Aren't the major events of God's plan of salvation clearly spelled out in Scripture? Don't the teaching passages of God's Word make salvation clear even without the interpretation of Old Covenant days? Must we insist, as some still do, that we must understand and observe certain days in order to understand salvation and to be saved? You will search in vain to find that idea in the New Testament.

Think about Paul's statement in I Corinthians 2:2 for a moment, "For I determined not to know anything among you except Jesus Christ and Him crucified."

What did Paul need in order to preach God's gospel of salvation at Corinth? Jesus Christ *and* the true meaning of each of the sabbaths and annual festivals? Jesus Christ *and* the law of Moses? Jesus Christ *and* the prophecies of future events in God's plan? No! Paul needed nothing "except Jesus Christ and Him crucified"!

Let's ask ourselves where we got this idea that understanding certain days is essential for salvation? Not from the Bible! Possible prophetic interpretations of the sabbaths and holy days may indeed be helpful and interesting, but let's all recognize that they are also a bit speculative and often go beyond what the Bible actually says. Let me give you a good example of this.

According to Mr. Armstrong's interpretation of the Feast of Tabernacles, the church always said that this week-long fall festival pictured the millennial reign of Christ over all the nations in the world tomorrow. Now there may be much truth to that suggestion. It is an interesting and attractive possibility, but at the same time I also recognize that this is *not* what the Bible says the Feast of Tabernacles means or how it interprets dwelling in booths or tents.

To find the Bible's own interpretation of the Feast of Tabernacles, all we need to do is turn to Leviticus 23:42-44:

"'You shall dwell in booths for seven days. All who are native Israelites shall dwell in booths, that your generations may know that I made the children of Israel dwell in booths *when I brought them out of the land of Egypt*: I am the Lord your God.' So Moses declared to the children of Israel the feast of the Lord."

What meaning does the Bible assign to the Feast of Tabernacles? *Israel's coming out of Egypt!* What meaning did Herbert Armstrong assign to the Feast of Tabernacles? "The Wonderful World Tomorrow" of Christ and the saints ruling over the nations for a thousand years. In the Worldwide Church of God, we seldom, if ever, heard about the meaning *that God himself* assigned to the festival. I admit, Mr. Armstrong's interpretation of the Feast of Tabernacles may be right; but I also recognize that his speculations about the holy days often overshadow the simple explanations of them that the Bible actually gives.

It is important to distinguish between what is interesting, attractive and speculative, and what is clearly stated in the Bible and is backed by Scriptural authority. For Paul, the sabbaths, new moons, and festivals were "shadows of things to come." That fact is in our Bibles, and is not speculation. And the "things to come" indeed *had come* in Christ. This, too, is established by the Bible, God's Word.

Paul did not attempt to stretch the meaning of the holy days into the future and cast their shadows to events yet to come, as did Herbert Armstrong. For Paul, the term shadow was an accurate and meaningful way to describe the Old Covenant holy days. He was comfortable with that term and all of its implications as it applied to the days and new moons required by the law of Moses. I am coming to be comfortable with it, too, little by little. I hope you are as well.

Paul knew when he wrote the book of Colossians that Christ was the very image and substance, the true reality indicated and anticipated by all the sabbath days, new moons, and festivals. Let us all rejoice in the Reality and no longer insist on celebrating the shadows.

Chapter Twelve

Common Sense
About Galatians

"You observe days and months and seasons and years. I am afraid for you, lest I have labored in vain" (Galatians 4:10-11). Here is another verse in the New Testament about observing days. But the question is, *what days*?

In Colossians 2:16 the days spoken of as shadows were clearly specified as sabbaths, new moons, and annual festivals. These are the days of the Old Covenant, and are commonly referred to as "the Jewish holidays." But the exact nature of the days mentioned in Galatians is not quite as obvious.

Those who believe that these Old Covenant days are no longer binding and required of Christians today usually identify them as the days of the Jewish sacred calendar. But those who believe these days are commanded for us today will insist that the days spoken of in Galatians must be some kind of pagan, Gentile holidays. They would argue that the sacred days of the Old Testament must be observed and defended, and that pagan holidays must be rejected. Their argument is captured in the title of Herbert Armstrong's booklet <u>Pagan Holidays—Or God's Holy Days—Which?</u>

Though there is little hard evidence to support them, many original and imaginative schemes have been proposed over the years in an attempt to make the days of

Galatians 4 into pagan days. Some of these speculations try to link the Galatians to a strict, Dead Sea cave-dwelling sect of the Jews called Essenes and to explain their practices as a strange blend of Jewish and Gentile beliefs.

I do not wish to examine those speculations here because, in the end, that is all they are or ever will be—speculations. But I would like to highlight the Biblical evidence we do have from Galatians and related passages. With that, and the application of a little common sense, I think we will see that the days spoken of in Galatians are the same days Paul spoke of in Colossians.

In this chapter I will show you how all the evidence points to their identity as Jewish, not pagan, Gentile holidays. I will also show you why some of our traditional Worldwide Church of God arguments to the contrary were sadly mistaken.

First, let's notice that nothing about Galatians 4:10 precludes us from identifying these days as the festivals of the Old Testament. All of the terms used in this verse are applicable to the days and events of the Jewish sacred calendar.

Certainly there were *days* commanded in the law of Moses—weekly and annual sabbath days. Certain *months* were especially important. All but one of the annual festivals fell in either the first or the seventh month. New moons were also observed in this sacred lunar calendar.

The festivals were all *seasonal* and were kept in the spring and fall, corresponding to the early and late harvest seasons. And there were special *years* as well in the sacred calendar—the land sabbath came every seven years and the Year of Jubilee was to be observed by Israel every fifty years.

So nothing about Galatians 4:10 rules out the days of the Jewish calendar. To the contrary, the language of that verse points toward those days, months, seasons, and years. But there is much more to examine in Galatians than merely the wording.

There are major spiritual issues at stake in Galatians; controversies abound. The central debate repeated over a dozen times is, of course, circumcision. The recently converted Gentile Christians in Galatia were being influenced by certain teachers who wanted them to be circumcised, a circumstance which Paul vigorously combats throughout the book (see especially Gal. 5:1-12).

Here is where we can begin to apply some common sense. If you knew that the Galatians had come under the spell of teachers promoting circumcision, what days do you *logically* suppose would be under discussion in this epistle? What days would you imagine such teachers were requiring of these new converts?

In Chapter 1:13-14, Paul identifies himself as someone formerly very advanced in "Judaism" (NIV, NKJV) or "the Jews' religion" (KJV). This is the only place in the New Testament where this phrase is used, and there is a reason why he refers to the Jewish religion. By this reference, Paul is stating his credentials and his "right," if you will, as a former Pharisee and teacher of the law, to engage in the arguments and issues facing the Galatians, all of which had their origins in Judaism.

Circumcision was no doubt the most Jewish of all the Jewish concerns along with keeping the law of Moses (Acts 15:5), and both are prominently discussed in Galatians. But Paul never refers to any pagan influences in this book as he does, for example, in I Corinthians. Meat offered to idols was clearly a pagan issue as was the sexual immorality associated with idolatry. We find these discussed in considerable detail in I Corinthians 6, 8, and 10. But there are no pagan issues before us in Galatians, only Jewish issues such as circumcision and justification by law.

The Galatians held the law of Moses in very high regard. They evidently believed the law was essential for justification, an idea Paul refutes in Galatians 2:16-17. He tries to check their enthusiasm for the law by asking them this question, "Did you receive the Spirit by works of the law, or by the hearing of faith?" (Gal. 3:2).

And in the next chapter, which includes a reference to the days they were observing, we find this question posed, "Tell me, you who desire to be under the law, do you not hear the law?" (Gal. 4:21). The Galatians wanted to be "under the law," a phrase that appears five times in this book.

It is time once again to apply a little common sense. What days would you suppose people would be observing who wanted to be "under the law"? Would people persuaded of the necessity of being under the law—even to the point of being circumcised—choose the days of the Jewish sacred calendar and law of Moses? Or would they prefer pagan, Gentile days? Which makes better sense, in your opinion?

Do you see why all the evidence points one way? It begins to strain all logic and common sense to force pagan days into Galatians which, as much as any other book in the New Testament, is devoted to Jewish issues.

But there is yet more evidence to consider. The language of Galatians links it inescapably to Acts 15 which also deals with circumcision and the law of Moses.

The false teachers of Galatia "troubled" the new Christians with their teaching. Notice in Gal. 1:7, "But there are some who trouble you," and also Gal. 5:10, "He who troubles you shall bear his judgment."

The word "troubled" links Galatians with Acts 15 and the Jerusalem Conference. Remember how James worded his letter to the Gentiles in Acts 15:24, "Since we have heard that some who went out from us have *troubled* you with words, unsettling your souls, saying,'You must be circumcised and keep the law'—to whom we gave no such commandment."

And recall James' advice about circumcision and the law of Moses, "We should not *trouble* those from among the Gentiles who are turning to God" (Acts 15:19).

"Troubling" new believers in both Acts 15 and Galatians means insisting on circumcision and the law of Moses for salvation. Can anyone show where this word is used to mean the teaching of pagan ways or pagan days? No. The word is never used with reference to pagan teachings.

Let's look now at how the term "yoke" is used in Galatians. Paul pleads with the Galatians, "Stand fast therefore in the liberty by which Christ has made us free, and do not be entangled again with a yoke of bondage" (Gal. 5:1).

The only other passage where yoke is similarly used is Acts 15:10. Peter, referring to the law of Moses, asks the assembled council of ministers, "Why do you test God by putting a yoke on the neck of the disciples which neither our fathers nor we were able to bear?"

The thought and language of Acts 15 and Galatians are so similar that most commentators state that they are both products of the same time and historic circumstances. Some scholars date Galatians a little before Acts 15; others, a little later, but almost all consider them closely linked.

Once again, common sense prompts us to ask some questions about the days mentioned in Galatians in light of the book's connection with Acts 15. Are there any pagan days or customs under consideration in Acts 15? No, only Jewish issues and concerns—Jewish Christians requiring circumcision and the law of Moses of new Gentile converts. Nothing in the parallel wording in Acts 15 would cause us to look for pagan days and customs in Galatians. The issues in both Acts 15 and Galatians are exclusively Jewish in origin.

But for the sake of argument, let's allow that the Galatians were somehow keeping pagan days, months, seasons, and years. And let's assume that Paul, like Herbert Armstrong in our day, insisted on the observance of the days of the Jewish sacred calendar. What would we then expect Paul to say about that strange state of affairs? What do you think Paul would say to recent converts who were mixing together the worst features of Judaism and paganism?

What if the Galatians wanted to be circumcised and under the law, and at the same time wanted to observe pagan days? Would Paul then simply say, "You observe days, months, seasons, and years"? Or would that most unusual blend of ideas not demand some further comment? Wouldn't Paul have called this contradictory blend of beliefs to their attention?

That is what Herbert Armstrong did in <u>Pagan Holidays—Or God's Holy Days—Which?</u> He said, in effect, "You're keeping the wrong days, the pagan days. Keep the right days, the good days, God's days."

But Paul doesn't do this. If they were keeping pagan days and Paul was trying to defend Jewish days, we should expect Paul to be saying, "Get your days right! You don't have to be circumcised or be under the law of Moses, but you do have to observe the Jewish calendar and keep those days. You've got it all backwards, you crazy Galatians! You insist on circumcision and the law of Moses and have lost the one thing you should have kept—the right days!"

But there is nothing in Galatians or anywhere else to suggest that Paul is addressing a strange amalgamation of pagan and Jewish practices. All the evidence we have of this early history of the Christian church is that teachers with Jewish notions and beliefs were demanding Jewish practices of new Gentile converts at Antioch, Galatia, and elsewhere.

Forcing unidentifiable pagan holidays and customs into Galatians is nowhere suggested and runs contrary to the evidence we do find there. And, nothing anywhere else in the Bible even hints of the possibility that Galatians 4:10 contains a reference to pagan days.

But, some will surely ask, what about the fact that Paul identifies the Galatians as former pagan idol worshippers in chapter 4, verse 9, and says they are *turning back* again to certain days? "How can pagans turn back again to Jewish days?" In the Worldwide Church of God this has always been our argument against the possibility that these might indeed be the days of the Old Covenant sacred calendar. "You can't turn back to something if you never were a part of it," right?

No, not right. Let's see why. Paul used precisely the same language in Galatians 5:1-2 when he spoke to these same Gentile converts about circumcision and the "yoke of bondage." Here it is once again, "...do not be entangled *again* with a yoke of bondage...I say to you that if you become circumcised, Christ will profit you nothing."

If we were following traditional Worldwide Church of God reasoning, we would have to argue with Paul and tell him that these uncircumcised Gentiles can't possibly be entangled *again* in circumcision because they never were circumcised in the first place! But from Paul's perspective, to revert back to the law of Moses and its various requirements was, figuratively speaking, to go *backward*. Backward in what way? To the *Old* Covenant! Now that Christ had come and Christianity had superseded Judaism, to go back to circumcision and the law of Moses was a step in the wrong direction whether you were a Jew or a Gentile. After Christ came, no one needed to go back again to the religious forms and practices of Judaism, which were now *obsolete*.

In Galatians 6, Paul again admonishes the Galatians to avoid "going back" and becoming entangled again in practices such as circumcision. We in the Worldwide Church of God said this entanglement did not and could not refer to the Gentiles' observance of Old Testament days. We appropriated a narrow, literal interpretation, when it is clear Paul was speaking in broad, figurative terms.

Dear reader, I am embarrassed to say I learned these arguments, I used these arguments, and I taught these arguments. Like so many others, I never seriously questioned them, challenged them, or diligently sought to prove them, until recently.

Time and again, when I put arguments like these to the test of God's Word, they fail. I am forced to recognize that what we engaged in so often in the past was not proof but a kind of indoctrination.

Now when I read Galatians 4:10 and put aside my former objections and prejudices, I see something completely different. I see that the Apostle Paul, the one who brought the Gospel to the Galatians, was deeply concerned that newly converted Christians were putting so much emphasis on the observance of Old Covenant days. I see Paul combatting what is merely another form of legalism. Getting caught up in days, seasons, months, and years, even if they were commanded under the law of Moses, misses the point just as much as getting focused on foods and meats.

I also see that what Paul says in Galatians bears a logical relationship to what he says in Colossians, which one would expect, of course, but something I could not see until recently. Before now, Paul's statements on days seemed to bear no relationship one to another. Now they do, and I am gratified to understand the connection between these passages on days.

We have one more passage on the subject to consider in the next chapter, which will bring us to a logical endpoint on the topic of sacred days.

Difficult Scriptures

Chapter Thirteen

Doubtful Disputations

We come now to the last passage in which Paul discusses the observance or non-observance of days. One would expect that all of Paul's statements on days would, like his teaching on meats, "speak the same thing," and that their relationship would be logical and obvious. Our previous attempts in the Worldwide Church of God to explain these passages never achieved this. We never saw a unity to Paul's teaching on days, which is not to say that our former ideas about these passages in Colossians, Galatians, and Romans didn't have, for us at least, a common theme.

What we always agreed upon in advance was that no matter what Paul might say in these verses, it would not diminish our belief that observing the sabbaths and annual festivals was mandatory for Christians. We never entertained the notion that these "difficult scriptures" could "do away with" the sabbaths, and therefore we saw no need to explore whether Paul's various statements revealed any unity of thought or common purpose.

With no more than this premise to guide us, the sabbaths, festivals, and new moons—called "shadows" in Colossians— were interpreted as foreshadowing yet future events in God's plan of salvation. The days Paul is surprised to find the Galatians observing we believed to be pagan, Gentile holidays, even though the entire book is about Jewish legalism. And the days of Romans 14, about which Paul simply says everyone should be fully persuaded his own mind, we arbitrarily declared to be "fast days."

So following our former teaching, all of Paul's statements on days point in different directions. In one instance, where the fact is inescapable, they are identified as Old Testament days. In another, they are called pagan days even in the context of Jewish legalism. And in a third, they are declared to be fast days even though there is no mention of fasting in the passage or any reason to believe fasting was a source of controversy.

What an interesting doctrinal state of affairs. Why is it that every time Paul speaks about the observance of days, they are always different days? What if there was some way of looking at all his statements on the subject that found them in harmony? What if they are, in fact, all talking about the same thing? Wouldn't that make much better sense than believing Paul is referring to completely different days every time he puts his pen to the subject?

The truth is that when Paul's statements on days are properly understood, he is in fact always "speaking the same thing" (the principle he himself expected of others in I Cor. 1:10), but applying and adapting his remarks to the local circumstances. At first Paul's statements to the Romans may seem different from those he made to the Colossians and Galatians, but that is because, as I will explain, the circumstances at Rome were very different and required a different tone and language.

Let's look at Paul's last statement on days and consider it in the light of the situation he faced at Rome. His advice to the Christians there was, "One person esteems one day above another; another esteems every day alike. Let every man be fully persuaded in his own mind" (Rom. 14:5).

Clearly this is different from "You observe days!" in Gal. 4:10 and "a shadow of things to come" in Col. 2:17.

Paul had an opinion about days that he openly expressed to the Colossians and Galatians. What accounts for the apparent neutrality and caution we find here in Romans? And for his uncharacteristic change in tone when he speaks to them about days?

What the Worldwide Church of God said in the past, of course, was that these days were not sabbaths and festivals, but fast days. I distinctly recall how this often was stated: "These *are* fast days because..." or "These *have to be* fast days because...." We had a knack for arbitrarily declaring verses, passages, and whole books to have a certain meaning— one that always conveniently fit our doctrinal paradigm. Following Herbert Armstrong's early example, and as we saw in his treatment of Colossians 2:16, we didn't always *prove* a text's meaning so much as *declare* its supposed meaning.

But why do these days "have to be" fast days? In the past we said they were fast days because eating "all things" (that is, meat) vs. vegetarianism was under discussion in the context surrounding Rom. 14:5, so obviously the days must have some connection with food and eating, or in this case, some kind of dietary restrictions, and *not* eating. Hence, these must be fast days!

It is amazing how little proof it takes to convince people to believe what they already want to believe. Because of an inability to face the fact that Paul was leaving the observance of days up to the individual believer, we were willing to declare the days of Romans 14 fast days on the slimmest of evidence and with virtually no proof. The topics of days and foods in this chapter are indeed connected, but much more logically than the sketchy and innovative interpretation we leaned on in the past had us believe.

To understand why Paul discusses foods and days together in Romans 14, let's briefly review the background of Romans. The first record of Roman Christians, or at least Romans who might have become Christians, is found in Acts 2. Among Peter's audience on that first Pentecost were "visitors from Rome, both Jews and proselytes." Now Jewish proselytes were Gentiles who had been circumcised as evidence of their faithfulness to the law. They were very zealous believers who forsook paganism to follow the teachings of Moses.

It is probably safe to assume that some of those Jews and devout proselytes were among the three thousand "who gladly received his word and were baptized" (Acts 2:41). These newly converted brethren with strong Jewish leanings then went back and became the nucleus of the Christian church at Rome.

But Paul wrote his epistle to the church at Rome nearly 25 years later. There is much internal evidence that the church had grown over the years and that many Gentiles had been added to the original core of Jewish and proselyte members. The Gentiles, by this point, probably outnumbered the Jewish members in the church. Many things had changed over the years, partly as a result of the Conference at Jerusalem which had removed the requirements of the law of Moses.

Paul knew many of the members of the Roman congregation by name and personally greeted dozens of them in Chapter 16. He also mentions several relatives, two of which, Andronicus and Junia, were converted before Paul, and who may have been among the original members of the Roman congregation (Rom. 16:7,11).

So Paul knew a lot about the church at Rome and probably kept in touch through his relatives who were now members of this fledgling congregation. Yet, he had never been to Rome or seen the Italian members face to face. In Roman 1:13 he laments the fact that he often planned to visit them, but was never able to make the trip a reality. He was, as the apostle to the Gentiles, eager to preach the gospel in what was the capital and most important city in the Roman Empire (Rom. 1:13,15).

Paul is keenly aware that he did not raise up this congregation and that this group of outlying Christians had, for the most part, maintained themselves on their own. He speaks of wanting to "establish" them in Rom. 1:11, as though no one officially had done so before.

So one of the reasons Paul's tone is somewhat moderate and only mildly corrective is that he was sensitive to his somewhat distant and tentative relationship with this congregation. As a Gentile church, they may have been within his jurisdiction, but many of their original members were Jews and proselytes who may have felt more of a bond with Peter and James than they did with Paul. We may also be certain that Paul prefers not to say or do anything that could potentially polarize or divide this community of believers.

Paul, in a fair and even-handed manner, addresses both the Jewish and Gentile communities within the Roman church, and demonstrates considerable insight into their respective problems and concerns.

He begins his epistle by addressing the Gentiles on the matters of idolatry and immorality (1:18-25), and in chapter two he speaks directly to the Jews, "Indeed you are called a Jew, and rest on the law, and make your boast in God." Paul acknowledges the advantages of being a Jew in chapter 3:1-2. He concludes that both Jews and Gentiles are under sin in chapter 3:9, and declares that the whole world is guilty before God (3:19). Returning to Jewish issues in chapters 9-11, Paul expresses his deep concern for his Israelitish countrymen and his great desire to see them saved (10:1; 11:1).

So there are both Jewish and Gentile converts at Rome, and Paul in his letter speaks knowledgeably to both communities. This mixed audience and the need to carefully address them both is one of the special features of the epistle to the Romans. Galatians and Colossians were written to predominantly Gentile congregations; Hebrews evidently was written to Jews in and around Jerusalem. But at Rome, Paul is dealing with an integrated church of both Jews and Gentiles who have fellowshipped with one another for years and who are trying to grow together in the faith. His even-handedness throughout is doubtless a sincere attempt not to side with one group over the other and expresses a keen sensitivity for their respective problems and concerns.

This background helps set the stage for Romans 14 and sheds considerable light on Paul's tone and intent. We already know there are two principle groups at Rome. In Romans 14 we discover that there is an additional two-fold division on the issues and attitudes in the congregation. There are people who eat "all things" and others who, for certain reasons, eat only vegetables. And there are people who highly esteem certain days and observe them unto the Lord, and there are others who do not. There are some who are "weak in faith" and others who are strong. And there are some who have a tendency to judge their fellow Christians, and others whose tendency is to belittle or despise their brethren.

The logical question is: could the polarizing tendencies of the brethren in Rome be linked to the Jewish/Gentile makeup of the congregation? The answer to that question is yes. There is abundant information to suggest that the food and days discussion in Romans 14 is the result of the understandably divergent views the Jews and Gentiles had concerning these matters.

In order to shed some sorely needed light on this chapter, I will be referring to James D.G. Dunn's exhaustive treatment of Romans 14 found in The Word Commentary, Volume 38, Romans 9-16. Section G of this volume is entitled "The Particular Problem of Food Laws and Holy Days" (Romans 14:1-15:6). In my opinion, Dunn's explanations stand head and shoulders above other attempts to explain this passage.

It seems that most commentators miss the obvious connection between dietary practices and what days should be kept. Historically, these were always matters of great importance and sensitivity to the Jews as well as for Jewish Christians.

Romans 14 opens with these words, "Receive one who is weak in the faith, but not to disputes over doubtful things." What are these "doubtful things" that are in dispute? Not surprisingly, foods and days. Some things never change, do they? Nearly 2,000 years later people are still disputing over the doubtful matters of foods and days.

Religious scruples are the basis of these disputes. Summing up the discussion in Romans 15:1, Paul says, "We then who are strong ought to bear with the scruples of the weak, and not to please ourselves." So what links foods and days here is not a common concern for eating or not eating certain foods on certain days, but is that these issues are *matters of conscience* for some people but not for others.

Now, among the members we know were at Rome, which group was most likely to have scruples about foods and days? Obviously, the long-time Jewish members, such as Paul's relatives and the former zealous Jewish proselytes. Speaking of the Jewish investment in the food issue, Dunn writes,

Too little appreciated in discussion of the passage is the considerable importance of dietary laws for Jews of this period. It was not simply that the laws of clean and unclean food were so clearly stated in the Torah....Also and even more important was the fact that the Maccabean crisis had made the observance of these laws a test of Jewishness, a badge of loyalty to covenant and nation....

That is to say, dietary rules constituted one of the clearest boundary markers which distinguished Jews from Gentiles and which were recognized as such; so also observance of the sabbath.[1]

Paul already had taken an active lead in lifting such food restrictions from the Gentile Christian community, and his statements on days did little to preserve their practice. "It was precisely this departure from such widely recognized social norms and identity markers," adds Dunn, "that must have caused considerable heart searching and dispute...among Jewish Christians and those previously most influenced by Jewish traditions."[2]

Jewish Christians at Rome undoubtedly had heard that the ministerial Conference at Jerusalem ruled that Gentile converts were not bound to the law of Moses, but that would not have settled the question entirely for them. Nor would it have made them feel free to violate long-standing habits practices and that had become, to them, matters of conscience.

To avoid the possibility of ritual defilement through contact with Gentile foods that were either unclean, improperly bled, or ceremonially defiled, many Jews simply "ate only vegetables." "Certainly wherever there was a fear of breaching the important sequence of food laws, the simplest and safest course would be to avoid meat altogether."[3] Vegetarianism for religious reasons was a practice dating back over six centuries to Daniel and his three friends in Babylon.

Bible students will recall that "Daniel purposed in his heart that he would not defile himself with the portion of the king's delicacies...therefore he requested of the chief of eunuchs that he might not defile himself" (Dan.1:8). Daniel's decision anticipates long in advance what some Jewish Christians at Rome would later do in order to avoid defilement, "Let them give us vegetables to eat and water to drink" (Dan. 1:12). Daniel's request was honored in that "the steward took away their portion of delicacies and the wine they were to drink, and gave them vegetables" (Dan. 1:16).

So vegetarianism had a long-standing Biblical history and would have been an attractive option to Roman Christians with Jewish scruples. This issue of eating all things versus eating only vegetables is best understood in this light, and again follows the principle of letting the Bible explain the Bible. Defilement by meats was a matter of religious scruples to some at Rome as it still is for some today. Paul honors and respects those scruples, but he does not try to elevate scruples about Old Covenant food laws to the level of "essentials" for all Christians.

The concern some Roman Christians had for days is best understood and explained in the same way. Those most likely to esteem certain days to the Lord were the Jewish Christians. Dunn regards the two issues of food and days as "all of a piece." He shows from detailed citations of Josephus, Philo, Juvenal, and other historic sources how the two issues were always considered by the Jews as hallmarks of covenant loyalty.

So is Paul really talking about fast days in Romans 14:5 as sabbatarians believe and we formerly taught in the Worldwide Church of God? No, as Dunn explains,

> The most obvious reference for v.5 is to a concern on the part of some Jewish Christians and others who had been proselytes or God-worshipers lest they abandon a practice of feast days and sabbath commanded by scripture and sanctified by tradition....This makes better sense than assuming a reference to fast days as such.[4]

It certainly makes better sense to me, and I trust it does to you as well. Here at last is an explanation of Romans 14 that not only fits the circumstances of the Book of Romans but also harmonizes with Paul's other statements on days recorded in his other epistles.

Paul walked a fine line between the scrupulous Jewish members with tender consciences concerning meats and days and Gentile members who had no such pangs of conscience and may have despised those who did. Paul appreciated the concerns of both groups. To him, they were all Christians whom he fervently desired would continue to walk together in unity and love. In the end, he leaves both matters to the choice of the individual member. Neither issue is viewed as something the church must decide and make binding one way for all Christians.

But there is more to be learned from this passage. Whom did Paul regard as the "weak in faith"? The rather surprising answer is that it was those with the tender scruples—"he who is weak eats only vegetables" (14:2).

And who is the one more likely to judge his brother? The vegetarian—"let not him who does not eat judge him who eats" (14:3).

Is this not true to human nature? Ironically, persons with very "high standards" in religious matters are often perceived by others (and perhaps by themselves as well) to be the "strong" Christians. They are admired for their discipline and uncompromising character. They can be counted on to defend the faith against laxness and compromise by weaker souls who do not hold to the same rigid principles.

But Paul, reversing the usual notions about character and righteousness, calls them "weak," and the persons who permit themselves to "eat all things" the "strong". (Paul includes himself among the strong in 15:1—"we who are strong"—so he, too, evidently must have eaten all things.)

How can this be? For one thing, those who ate all things seemed to have a more mature understanding of essentials and non-essentials. Faithful adherence to Old Covenant requirements did not—does not—make one a better or a stronger Christian. Rather, overemphasizing the non-essentials like foods and days often subtracts from a right relationship with God and fellow man. In this case, the avidly scrupulous were more inclined to judge their brethren, something that continues to this day in many religious circles. Simply stated, legalism often makes for self-righteousness. And self-righteousness takes its toll on human relations.

Paul's primary focus in this important passage clearly was not on foods and days but on unity, peace, and right ways of relating in the church—especially between Jews and Gentiles. His advice was that neither should judge or despise the other. He gives compelling reasons why they should accept and receive one another, "for God has received him...Therefore, whether we live or die, we are the Lord's" (14:3, 8). Meat-eaters and vegetarians, day observers and non-day observers are all brethren whom God has received in Christ, so Christians must do the same.

Paul's words echo Peter's earlier declaration in Acts 15:8-9, "So God, who knows the heart, acknowledged them by giving them the Holy Spirit just as He did to us, and made no distinction between us and them." Both Peter and Paul knew and emphatically taught that the formerly binding restrictions and regulations of the law of Moses were no longer grounds for judging and rejecting others whom God had clearly accepted.

Paul called the issues of foods and days "doubtful matters," and he treated them as non-essentials. And he taught that on such issues "each of us shall give account of himself to God" (14:12). His principle exhortation and ultimate concern is clearly stated in Romans 14:13, "Therefore let us not judge one another anymore." Would that every Christian resolved to do just that and treat these doubtful matters with the same wisdom and tolerance.

Administrative Policy on Foods and Days

What we are given in Romans 14 is a divinely inspired policy statement on the twin issues of meats and days. Some may wish to quibble on the fine points of Paul's doctrine, but the policy that Paul administered in the Church of God is clear beyond doubt. Under the direction of the Chief Shepherd, Jesus Christ, Paul leaves the matters of meats and days up to the individual's choice.

156

As Turner in the Wesleyan Bible commentary observes,

> Some questions cannot be settled on
> the basis of human consensus. They must be
> handled as matters of conscience—the soul
> witnessing to itself that one is acting on the
> best knowledge he has after every effort has
> been made to ascertain the truth....More fun-
> damental than the correctness of one's con-
> clusions in matters of non-essentials is one's
> attitude toward God.[5]

And just how did Paul administer the food and day issues in the church? Was anyone ever *commanded* to observe a certain day? Or told with authority *not to eat* a certain food? Was anyone at any time ever disciplined or disfellowshipped for failure to observe any such regulations?

Was anyone told that the sabbath or holy days were "a test commandment"? Ellen G. White called the sabbath "a testing truth" for Christians in the last days. Herbert Armstrong in his early writings called it "the final test of obedience." Where does the New Testament make the sabbath a special test, or sign, or insist on its observance as essential for believers?

Was anyone in the New Testament ever told that certain foods and certain days were essential for salvation? No, you won't find any New Testament writer making a test commandment out of the sabbath or making it binding for all believers. You will, however, find the essentials for inheriting the Kingdom of God in I Corinthians 6:9-10, but no mention of food or days there. No passage of the New Testament makes such matters binding and required on Christians.

Bruce's comments captures the New Testament teaching on matters of conscience versus matters of obligation,

> The observance of the sacred calendar, like the observance of the levitical food laws, was obligatory on Jews. But Christians are free from obligations of this kind. If a Christian decides to abstain from certain kinds of food and drink, or to set aside certain days or seasons for special observance, commemoration, or meditation, good: these are questions to be settled between the individual conscience and God...But to regard them as matters of religious obligation is a retrograde step for Christians to take.[6]

The only policy that Paul ever administered concerning these matters is stated in Romans 14:5, "One person esteems one day above another; another esteems every day alike. Let each be fully persuaded in his own mind." That is still the best policy. It came from God. No man and no church will ever improve upon it. Would that it were the policy of every church to do the same.

Are you fully convinced in your own mind what you should do concerning meats and days? If you are, good! I respect your convictions and beliefs. And I hope you honor mine as well.

But if you are not fully convinced about what you should do, then I encourage you to study and pray about it until you are fully persuaded. But regardless what our different convictions may be, "let us not judge one another anymore," but let us live with one another in love, joy, and peace.

Putting It All Together

Now that we've covered Paul's individual passages on days, let's put them together and see how they fit as a whole. To do this properly, we'll need to arrange them in chronological order.

The three statements we examined span approximately the same period Luke describes in the last half of the Book of Acts. Each comes from a different time in Paul's ministry. Laying them out chronologically helped me understand them more deeply.

"You observe days and months and seasons and years!" comes from Galatians, which was written early in Paul's ministry, soon after his first evangelistic journey through Asia Minor. It is possible that Galatians may be the first book of the New Testament to be written. Paul may have penned it as early as the late 40's AD, even before the Jerusalem Conference, which took place about 50 AD. That this epistle makes no mention of that historic conference in a letter devoted to the issue of Jewish legalism, is one reason why many authorities date it so early.

But Galatians, as noted earlier, parallels the time and circumstances of Acts 15. Paul and Peter were combating the legalistic ideas of the Jewish Christians and of other false teachers who insisted on circumcision and strict adherence to the law of Moses.

Paul's statement in Galatians 4:10 comes from this early time when Jewish problems were the subject of "no small dissension and dispute" (Acts 15:1-2). As I explained in Chapter 13, common sense alone would tell us that people who wanted to be circumcised and desired "to be under the law" would have wanted to keep whatever days were prescribed by that law. The Galatians were not

159

trying to blend circumcision with totally foreign and repugnant Gentile days such as Saturnalia.

Paul's earliest statement is one of shock coupled with deep concern—"I am afraid for you." Paul is genuinely amazed that these Gentile Christians were more caught up in calendar calculations than in Christ and the Spirit. He was expressing his gut reaction, not establishing a policy statement. This fresh and spontaneous emotional quality makes it sound like Paul's earliest response to the days dispute.

The statement on days in the book of Romans comes in the mid-50's AD and from a different time in his ministry. Paul was busy raising up and administrating large Gentile churches such as Corinth and Ephesus. It was after the Jerusalem Conference, and the principles decided by that conference were being administered in the churches under Paul's jurisdiction. When Paul spoke to the Romans about days, he had already given the matter a lot of thought. Romans 15:5 is not an emotional reaction. It is a policy statement that best served the needs of both the Jewish and Gentile Christians at Rome and that could be applied to Christians anytime, anywhere.

For Paul to have insisted on certain foods and days would have contradicted the principle of Christian liberty and offended the Gentile element of the Roman congregation. To have lightly dismissed the Old Covenant food laws and holy days would have offended the Jewish element and would have violated their religious scruples. Paul wisely does neither, but leaves both of these "disputes over doubtful things" (Rom. 14:1, NKJV) up to the conscience of each individual Christian. Thus, he gives the church the best possible administrative policy on matters that are not essential for salvation.

Lastly, Paul's statement on all the Old Covenant/law of Moses days found in Colossians, and which he calls shadows, comes from the time of his first Roman imprisonment. Colossians is one of the Prison Epistles and was probably written in the late 50's or early 60's AD.

In Colossians we have neither a fervent emotional reaction nor an administrative policy statement, but a more complete explanation of Paul's view of the days of the sacred calendar. It was written to a Gentile church clearly within his jurisdiction, and Paul doesn't feel the need to be overly cautious and diplomatic. It is most unlikely he would have called the sabbath days, new moons, and annual festivals "shadows" to the Romans, but he calls them just that in Colossians. He explains to the Colossian church and to those in the entire Ephesus region (see Col. 4:16) that these days were all "shadows of things to come," early indications of once future things that had now come to pass through Christ.

The wording is similar to Hebrews, which came from the same late stage in Paul's ministry. He began to speak in increasingly plain terms—even to the Jews regarding the Old Covenant's obsolescence (Heb. 8:13). Paul senses his ministry and life are coming to an end, and he does not spare the recipients of his epistles his opinions.

Putting all of these statements on a time line, we see that Paul's statements on days have a unity of thought and purpose but that each is a product of a different time and circumstance. We should not try to explain the differences by assuming that Paul is referring to three different kinds of days—Gentile days, Jewish days, and fasting days—as we formerly did in the Worldwide

Church of God. We would do far better to think of them as statements on the same days, but tailored to different audiences at different times in Paul's life and ministry.

I find this a far more logical and satisfying explanation of these passages than trying to make something different out each of them. Seen in this light, Paul follows his own good advice of "speaking the same thing."

In the next chapter we will take a closer look at the one day that is of the supreme importance to some Christians—the sabbath.

Chapter Fourteen

But What About the Sabbath?

I come now to a question put to me by a long-time friend and fellow minister who left our fellowship over these doctrinal differences and started his own church. I got together with him during a trip to California and we had dinner together at a nice restaurant as we often had in the past. He is a dear friend and a brother in Christ, and even though we see things differently these days, it would have been unthinkable for me to be in California and not look him up.

As I expected, our time together was full of warmth, affection, and good humor. Despite our recent differences, we are deeply bonded brothers and friends who well fulfill Proverbs 27:17, "Iron sharpens iron, so a man sharpens the countenance of his friend."

My friend spoke of the reasons that compelled him to leave the Worldwide Church of God and of the doctrines he was seeking to defend. Later in our conversation I could not help but ask him how he understood the matter of the law of Moses in light of the Jerusalem Conference of Acts 15. I have always respected him as a faithful student of God's Word and one who prizes good scholarship, so I was truly interested in his views. Somehow he seemed unable or unwilling to pursue the issue very far. It was as if, for him, it was not particularly important or relevant.

His response should have come as no surprise because, as I have explained, in our church we always diminished or dismissed the importance of the law of Moses. It never shaped our thinking or doctrine, except in a narrowly ritualistic or ceremonial sense.

My good friend was quick to redirect the conversation to the issue about which he was most concerned. Putting aside my question about the law of Moses, he came back with the question that was of greatest importance to him, "But, Dave, what about the sabbath?"

I knew what his question meant. In answering my question with a question, he was saying, in effect, "Let's not get side-tracked or bogged down in some minor details about the law of Moses. Let's get down to basics and the things that matter most. Surely you don't think the sabbath was affected by any of the changes in Acts 15 or anywhere else, do you?' Like so many who are deeply invested in Old Covenant thinking, the place he wanted to draw the line was at the sabbath.

That animated conversation, which went on not only until the restaurant closed, but continued a good while longer in the parking lot, was one of my major inspirations for writing this book. It is always hard to do justice to these giant issues of faith and doctrine in any one conversation. There is always so much to say and to consider.

Please understand that it is *far* beyond the scope of this book to discuss the issue of the sabbath comprehensively. What I purpose to do instead is to give you the principles that have shaped my own understanding about the sabbath. Think of them, if you wish, as Dave Albert's personal conclusions based on his own understanding of the Scripture.

Let's remember Paul's admonition about days in Romans 15:5. He said, "Let each be fully persuaded in his own mind." What follows are the scriptural principles about the sabbath of which I am fully persuaded. They may not fully persuade you, but I urge you to read them with a spirit of fair-mindedness.

Traditional sabbatarian defense of the sabbath rests on two main premises that you will see time and again in sabbatarian literature. The first of these is that the sabbath is found in the Ten Commandments and that nothing found in the Ten Commandments can be modified, rescinded, or done away.

The second defense of the sabbath is that it is part of God's moral law, and the moral law, unlike the ceremonial law, is eternal and cannot be changed. Hence, the sabbath stands forever.

I used to be convinced of this reasoning until I found that it is not supported by scripture. It sounds terribly weighty and convincing and would seem clearly beyond all contradiction, but those two oft-quoted ideas simply fall apart under close scrutiny, as I am about to show you.

Let's examine both of these sabbath defenses, first, from a sabbatarian point of view, and then from a Biblical point of view. Some of you may be surprised to learn that they are, in fact, two *opposing* positions.

The Seventh Day Adventist perspective on the sabbath is nicely summed up in their Seventh Day Adventist Bible Commentary's treatment of Colossians 2:16-17. That verse poses a potential problem for Adventists just as it did for Herbert Armstrong because it calls "a festival or a new moon or sabbaths" "a shadow of things to come."

In these verses Paul has completely removed the ground from beneath the feet of the Judaizing false teachers. They advocated a return to Judaic ceremonial requirements. The apostle meets their arguments by asserting that the shadows have served their function now that Christ, the reality, has come. In all this argument Paul is in no way minimizing the claims of the Decalogue or of the seventh-day Sabbath. The moral law is eternal and perfect.[1]

Obviously, the Adventists do not consider Paul's shadow metaphor applicable to the weekly sabbath, and they steer the reader away from that notion. Instead, they apply the metaphor to the annual festivals and new moons but not to the sabbath—*even though sabbath days are distinctly mentioned*—because the sabbath is part of the Decalogue—God's eternal, unchangeable, moral law.

This commentary also cites a Presbyterian scholar, who observes that Paul "had his eye on the great number of days which were observed by the Hebrews as festivals, as part of their ceremonial law, and not to the *moral* law (emphasis his), or the ten commandments ."[2]

The assumption here is that the Ten Commandments are an inviolable moral law and that, as such, they are not subject to modification. Let's see now how Herbert Armstrong defends the sabbath on this same ground in his booklet, Which Day Is the Sabbath of the New Testament?

In it Mr. Armstrong attempts to separate the law of Moses and the Ten Commandments. He comments specifically on Acts 15 and, as with his teaching on unclean foods, assures the reader that the sabbath is not part of the law of Moses. Under the subhead, "Gentiles Met on the Sabbath," he writes,

> *Acts 15:1-2, 5, 14-21*: Study this whole passage carefully. Certain men had come down from Judea to Antioch, teaching that the Gentile converts there must be circumcised and keep the law of Moses to be saved. Quite a dissention arose between them and Paul and Barnabas. So it was decided Paul and Barnabus should go to Jerusalem to the apostles and Elders (sic) about the question.
>
> At the conference at Jerusalem, James gave the decision. "Wherefore my sentence is," he pronounced, (verses 19-21), "...*that we write* unto them, that they abstain from pollutions of idols, and from fornication, and from things strangled, and from blood."
>
> He did not say they should not keep the Ten Commandments. The Ten Commandments were not in question—but only the Law of Moses, which was an altogether DIFFERENT law. He merely mentioned four prohibitions, and otherwise they did need to observe the law of Moses (emphasis Mr. Armstrong's throughout).[3]

Here again, for Mr. Armstrong as well as the Seventh Day Adventists, the best defense for the sabbath is its location in the Ten Commandments. For most sabbatarians an appeal to the Decalogue is all that is necessary. The logic of that argument seems airtight and beyond any question or doubt. "How," they might ask, "could anyone *possibly* believe otherwise?"

For starters, may I point out that this is an altogether human line of reasoning that is never used by anyone, at any time, any place in the Bible?

You may be surprised to learn that *the phrase "the Ten Commandments" cannot be found in the New Testament and that no New Testament writer or speaker ever seeks to support his position by appealing to the fact that something is found in the Ten Commandments.* To be sure, various of the Ten Commandments are mentioned in the New Testament, but no one ever refers to the Decalogue as an eternal legal code, as have Herbert Armstrong and the Seventh Day Adventists.

The term "Ten Commandments" does appear in the Old Testament, but I don't think the average sabbatarian knows how it actually is used in the Bible. I know I didn't until recently. If we are going to base one of our major sabbath arguments on "the Ten Commandments," shouldn't we know and use the term way the Bible does?

So how exactly does the Bible treat the term "the Ten Commandments"? Notice Exodus 34:27-28, the first of three places where it appears:

> "Then the Lord said to Moses, 'Write these words, for according to the tenor of these words I have made a covenant with you and with Israel.' So he was there with the Lord forty days and forty nights; he neither ate bread nor drank water. And he wrote on the tablets *the words of the covenant, the Ten Commandments.*"

So what in the Bible is the term "Ten Commandments" used to define? Eternal moral principles that can never be modified or changed? That is what many have said and written, but *the Bible* plainly says that the Ten Commandments are the very core and essence of the covenant God made with Israel at Mount Sinai.

We find this important truth repeated in Deuteronomy 4:11-14,

> "Then he came near and stood at the foot of the mountain, and the mountain burned with fire to the midst of heaven, with darkness, cloud, and thick darkness. And the Lord spoke to you out the midst of the fire. You heard the sound of the words, but saw no form; you only heard a voice. *So He declared to you His covenant which He commanded you to perform, that is, the Ten Commandments;* and He wrote them on two tablets of stone. And the Lord commanded me at that time to teach you statutes and judgments, that you might observe them in the land which you cross over to possess."

So, by "letting the Bible interpret the Bible," we see that the Ten Commandments, along with the statutes and judgments, were part of the covenant God made at Sinai with Israel through Moses. We have just read for ourselves precisely how the Bible uses the term "the Ten Commandments," and it is never used in Scripture *in any other way.* (The third and last reference to the Ten Commandments is found in Deut. 10:4 where Moses describes God's instructions for carrying the Commandments in the ark.) One may wish to assign other meanings, "special" meanings to the term, but to do so is scripturally insupportable human reasoning.

Now if the Old Covenant with its Ten Commandments, statutes, and judgments is eternal and still binding today, then there is no question that we should keep not only the sabbath but *everything else* found therein. But, of course, you see at once the problem with that idea. The New Testament makes it abundantly clear that the covenant God made with Israel at Sinai, the Old Covenant, is now obsolete, and has been superseded by the New Covenant, "In that he says, 'A new covenant,' He has made the first obsolete. Now what is becoming obsolete and growing old is ready to vanish away" (Heb. 8:13).

In Paul's day, when the Temple still stood and the priesthood administered sacrifices, Paul said that the Old Covenant was "ready to vanish away." Spiritually, it had already become obsolete by Christ's sacrifice and his establishment of the New Covenant by his blood, but when the Temple was destroyed in 70 AD, the last tangible remnant of the Old Covenant—the daily sacrifices— finally "vanished away".

So an appeal to "the Ten Commandments" as a defense of the sabbath is really nothing more than an appeal to the terms and conditions of the Old Covenant—a covenant that is obsolete and no longer binding. And that is why I am no longer "fully persuaded," as I once was, that the sabbath is obligatory just because it is a part of the Ten Commandments.

Jesus Christ, as the giver of the New Covenant, can modify or change *any* part of the Old Covenant according to his Father's will. The entire covenant is now obsolete. However, that does not mean all of its laws, commandments, and principles are obsolete. Many clearly came across into the New Covenant and are confirmed by much New Testament teaching. But no part of that Old Covenant is sacred and untouchable just because it appears in the Ten Commandments. Such an idea, to quote one of Herbert Armstrong's favorite expressions, "is simply not scriptural."

But what about the notion that the sabbath is part of God's eternal *moral law*? Doesn't that make it binding forever?

If you think that is true, may I point out something that I think you already know? The sabbath forbids for one day the very thing it enjoins on the other six. In the Fourth Commandment we are told that "Six days shall you labor and do all your work, but the seventh day is the Sabbath of the Lord your God. In it you shall do no work" (Ex. 20:9-10).

What kind of *moral* principle is that? One day of the week we are forbidden to do the very thing we should do on the other six? That is, indeed, a peculiar "eternal, moral law"!

It is clear that the Fourth Commandment is distinctly different from the other nine commandments, which forbid such things as idolatry, murder, adultery, theft, and lying. You cannot do those things six days a week and avoid them on the seventh. Lying is *always* wrong. So is adultery, murder, and theft. But work is forbidden on one day per week and commanded on the other six. Again, I ask, what kind of *moral* law is that?

Can we begin to see an essential difference between the sabbath and the other commands? The sabbath is much like the Day of Atonement on which eating and drinking were prohibited one day per year, even though food and drink are good, necessary, and permissible the other 364 days. Food isn't evil or bad of itself, but one day of the year it was forbidden.

How is it that we can proclaim a law moral and eternal that arbitrarily declares that which is otherwise necessary and good (work, food) to be unlawful for one day per week or one day per year? It should be apparent that such a law should properly be described as ceremonial and clearly is not based on any eternal, *moral* principle.

Jesus himself treated the sabbath as a ceremonial rather than a moral law in his actions and teaching. When his disciples plucked grain on the sabbath, they were accused of sabbath breaking by the Pharisees, who said to Jesus, "Look, why do they do what is not lawful on the sabbath?" Jesus' reply contains a reference to a ceremonial practice. He told them, "Have you never read what David did when he was in need and hungry, he and those with him; how he went into the house of God in the days of Abiathar the high priest, and ate shewbread, which is not lawful to eat?" (Mark 2:26).

Jesus likened the behavior of his disciples on the sabbath to that of David and his men, who, when hungry, ate the priest's shewbread. Was eating shewbread an eternal, moral principle? No, it was a ceremonial matter. The bread had a ceremonial use that could be waived in an emergency. Neither David and his men nor Jesus and his disciples were guilty of breaking a moral law. Ceremonies could be set aside, Jesus explained to the Pharisees, when there is a pressing human need.

Sacred day laws, like food laws, are ceremonial, not moral, in nature. They can be waived or modified if necessary. The sabbath law, unlike true spiritual and moral laws, had many exceptions. Priests were allowed to "profane" the sabbath (Matt. 12:5). Circumcisions could be performed on the sabbath (Mark 7:22-23). Even the work involved in caring for animals (Mark 13:15) or pulling a donkey or an ox out of a pit were permitted on the sabbath (Mark 14:5).

What kind of "eternal moral law" has so many exceptions? Does "Thou shalt not commit adultery" have exceptions? Or "Thou shalt not steal"? No, the Bible makes no exceptions for *truly* moral laws such as these.

After weighing the Biblical evidence, I have had to conclude that the sabbath is indeed a ceremonial matter, not a moral issue. It derived its authority from the Old Covenant God made with Israel, and was an important identifying sign of that Covenant (see Ex. 31:16-17). No one in the New Testament—other than the Jewish zealots and Pharisees, that is—treated the sabbath as an eternal moral principle.

We read in the gospels that the Jews repeatedly accused Jesus of sabbath violations. After he healed a man on the sabbath, they sought to kill him because he "broke the sabbath" (John 5:18). And in John 9:16 the Pharisees said, "This man is not from God, because He does not keep the Sabbath." How quick they were to judge the very Son of God (the Lord of the sabbath!) on this matter of the sabbath.

How did Jesus defend himself against these charges? Did he ever deny that he was working on the sabbath? No, he freely admitted that he was working. He said in response to their charges, "My Father has been working until now, and I have been working" (John 5:17). And on the sabbath he said, "I must work the works of him who sent me while it is day" (John 9:4).

Now could Jesus say that about a moral law? Could he say, "My Father and I have been lying until now"? Or, "I must be stealing today"? Of course not! Jesus' admission that he and his Father regularly worked on and thus "broke the sabbath" confirms for me that the sabbath is ceremonial. There clearly were times in Jesus' ministry when human needs such as hunger or healing could override a rigid, ceremonial observance of the sabbath law.

I have become "fully persuaded" in my study of God's Word that the sabbath is a ceremonial law. Perhaps that it is categorically ceremonial and not moral explains why it is never mentioned in any of the "sin lists" of the New Testament (Mark 7, I Cor. 6, Gal. 5).

It also explains why Paul says in Hebrews that the sabbath, is a "shadow of things to come." The ceremonial nature of the sabbath also explains why Peter and Paul did not insist on it for baptism or salvation and why they did not administer an official sabbath policy in the church other than "let every man be fully persuaded in his own mind." As noted in the previous chapter, we see no attempt by the apostles to administer either the ceremonial food laws or day laws.

Arguments from Silence

But some respond to this by saying, "That's just an argument from silence, and arguments from silence don't prove anything." Let's give that matter some serious thought. Is it true that an argument from silence proves nothing? I think we all pay attention to silences and we know instinctively that arguments from silence prove something. Let me give you a few examples.

Let's say you are watching a movie in a theater, and suddenly there is no sound. The picture is fine. You can still see the action on the screen, but you can't hear any dialogue. Up to that point there had been sound. Now, aside from the grumbling patrons, there is silence. What does it mean? What does it prove?

Or maybe you've been in a mountain cabin or in a ship at sea during a violent, noisy storm. Night came, and you went to sleep with the storm still raging. Sometime in the night you awoke and were aware that something was different. Then it occurs to you—the wind has subsided. It's quiet and calm. The storm is over. What did the silence "prove" to you?

Let me give you one last example. You're approaching a busy street or freeway during the rush hour—say 5:00 pm on a Friday afternoon. As you get closer you're struck by the fact that it's strangely quiet. You hear no horns honking, no cars and trucks rushing by, none of the usual traffic noises. What would the unexpected silence tell you?

In each of these experiences, you would quickly conclude that the sudden and unexpected silence meant that *something was different* and *some kind of significant change had occurred*. In each case you would have read meaning into the silence, interpreted it in some way. The silence would be instructive, and it would prove to you that something about the circumstance had changed.

Let's apply that principle to the administration of the sabbath in the Old and New Testaments. I can easily show you a dozen places in the Old Testament where the sabbath was enforced or administered through reproofs, threats, and warnings (see, for example, Ex. 16 and Neh. 13), as well as through the death penalty, as in the case of the man who was caught gathering sticks (Num. 13).

There is a lot of a consistent, uninterrupted activity and "sound" surrounding the enforcement of the sabbath in the Old Testament.

The Jews of Jesus' day, continuing this practice, accused Jesus and the disciples time and again of sabbath violations. They attempted to enforce sabbath observance and reproved anyone they thought was guilty of profaning the sabbath—including the crippled man Jesus healed at the Pool of Bethesda. He was admonished, "It is the sabbath; it is not lawful for you to carry your bed" (John 5:10).

Much vigorous teaching and enforcement activity surrounds the administration of the sabbath in both the Old and New Testaments—right up until the Old Covenant ends with the death and resurrection of Jesus Christ. Then suddenly, there is total silence.

No one ever again is commanded to keep the sabbath, warned about failure to observe the sabbath, or reproved or punished for sabbath violations. In the New Testament there is not so much as a whisper about the administration of the sabbath. What had been an enormous issue suddenly became a non-issue.

No one after Christ's resurrection is spoken of as "resting on the sabbath," or told how to properly observe the sabbath. I don't mean for a moment that no one observed or rested on the sabbath. That is not my point. My point is that the sabbath ceased to be an administrative concern in the New Testament.

Other matters received administrative attention and other laws certainly were enforced. Fornication and sexual immorality were strictly forbidden, and the sexually immoral person in I Corinthians 5 was reprimanded in the strongest possible manner. He was disfellowshipped by the Apostle Paul—put out of the church until he repented.

But while such moral precepts were conscientiously enforced and violators disciplined in the New Testament church, not *one word* is ever mentioned about sabbath or holy day violations. Clearly some kind of major change occurred concerning the sabbath. The silence is instructive to those who have ears to hear.

Let's not be quick to dismiss an argument from silence. Silence can and almost always does demonstrate or prove something. New Testament silence on the enforcement of sacred days and the food laws (along with clear instructional passages) helps establish the fact that both of these were treated as matters of individual conscience and choice. Neither is enjoined at any time on anyone as "an eternal moral law." I am therefore fully persuaded that neither food laws nor sacred day laws can be enjoined on believers today for baptism, church membership, or salvation. Nor should they be matters over which churches separate and divide.

When strict sabbatarians elevate the sabbath to a point of contention and division even to the point of splitting families and brethren, they are doing so entirely without scriptural authority and in plain contradiction of the far more important principles of peace, unity, love, and brotherhood. Recall that Paul could have easily split the Roman congregation by taking a stand on the food and day issues, but he wisely did not do so. Instead, he left these matters of conscience up to the individual.

So, "*What about the sabbath?*" I hope I have been clear about why I am fully persuaded on that matter, and what I have found in God's Word to substantiate my convictions. I hope you have found what I have said thought- provoking and Biblically based. But if you are fully persuaded otherwise—and I realize that some of you may be—then I respect the fact that what you are doing, you are doing "unto the Lord" (Rom. 14:6), and I respect your convictions and faith. In matters that Paul labels "doubtful things" in Romans 14:1, "each of us shall give account of himself to God" (vs. 12).

Personally, I still observe the sabbath. I need a weekly day of rest and the additional time the sabbath gives me for study, prayer, and meditation. It is the day on which we traditionally met and still meet in the Worldwide Church of God. The sabbath has many present benefits and is also rich with historic and prophetic meaning. I think of it as a most appropriate day for rest and worship, given its long history and tradition among the people of God.

So I am not in any way against the sabbath or sabbath observance, but I no longer think of the sabbath as a profound moral principle. I also permit myself a wider range of activities on the sabbath than I did in the past. I do not criticize those who keep the day differently than I do, nor those who observe a different day. I believe that is their choice, a matter of conscience for them to decide for themselves before God.

Personally speaking, I no longer want to be at odds with other believers over food choices or day choices, and I will happily give account to God and my Lord and Master Jesus Christ for this belief because I am certain it is based upon the principles of his Word.

In the next and final chapter, I will share with you some things that have helped me understand why God might exercise his prerogative to make changes in his laws at certain times and for specific purposes.

Chapter Fifteen

Pursuing the
Character Ideal

Well, dear reader, it is time to bring things to an end, or as Solomon said, to hear the conclusion of the matter.

In this concluding chapter I want to share with you a perspective that has helped me a great deal in recent months. Throughout this book I have been speaking about the law of Moses as something temporary, something that started with Moses and the children of Israel at Sinai and ended at the time of Christ. But as many of you know, there are prophecies that clearly suggest that much of this same law of Moses will be back in force in the Millennial reign of Christ. How do we explain this apparent contradiction?

I have said that some of the most notable features of the law of Moses such as the food and sacred day laws were *on* in the days of Moses, *off* in the days of Peter and Paul, especially after the Acts 15 conference, and then seem to be back *on* in the Kingdom era after Christ's return. Does that make sense? Or am I contradicting myself?

I must admit that for a long time that kind of "on/off/on" reasoning made no sense to me whatsoever. We always tended to believe in the Worldwide Church of God that God's law, like God himself, does not change. We would quote verses such as Hebrews 13:8, "Jesus Christ the same yesterday, today, and forever" to prove our point.

The idea of a whole law or legal code of God being temporary was foreign to our thinking. We believed that God requires much the same things of all people at all times. Following this line of reasoning, we would say, "If the sabbath and tithing and clean and unclean meats were required in the past and will be required in the future, surely they are required of us today."

We would argue against the "on/off/on" idea of legal requirements with the much simpler and more direct "on— in the *past*, on—in the *present*, on—in the *future*" argument that seemed to make better sense. That kind of reasoning about God's law seemed a lot more logical and consistent, and certainly more fair—one law, for all people, at all times.

And yet we always knew there were exceptions. Circumcision was not required of anyone before Abraham, hence, "off." Then it was required, at least of Israelites, and "on" until Christ came. Then after Acts 15 we know it was once again "off." On/*off*/on, again.

Animal sacrifices were *on* for Israel, are *off* for Christians today, and according to some prophecies, seem to be back *on* in the future. The same could be said of the land sabbaths, the death penalty, the Temple, and the priesthood. They all follow the pattern of "on/off/on." How can this be? How can God change his laws?

We surely know he changed the law of the priesthood because the Bible specifically says so in Hebrews 7:12, "For the priesthood being changed, of necessity there is also *a change of the law*." So we all have known at some level that law— even God's law—can change if and when necessary. But why?

Can we somehow come to understand the reason or reasons God has for changing his law? If we grasp God's logic for instituting the changes, we can better accept them and apply them to our lives.

What follows is my understanding of how certain features of God's law can be on in the past, off in the present, and then back on in the future. The rationale for such changes can best be explained, I think, if we contrast what I am going to call the "national and ceremonial ideal" with the "spiritual or character ideal." I think when we grasp the difference between these two ideals, we can better understand the changes in God's law that we find recorded in the Bible.

Let me give you the conclusion first so you'll know where I'm going, then I'll go back over the details. It seems clear to me from my studies of God's Word and from the insights I have gained from many of the better Bible commentators, that when God dealt with Israel, beginning in the days of Moses, he assigned many nationalistic purposes to the law. The law regulated, identified, and defined the nation of Israel to itself and to the rest of the world. Israel's identity was achieved in large part by many rituals and ceremonies such as, but by no means limited to, circumcision. Food and day laws were also a big part of Israel's identity.

In the time of the New Testament church and present Christian era, the law of God is not focused on a national purpose or ideal but on a personal character ideal exemplified and made possible by Jesus Christ. Understand that I do not mean character in the limited sense of willpower, but in the much broader sense of God's very nature in us, the "divine nature" of which we may be partakers, according to II Peter 1:4.

At this time God is not primarily concerned with a chosen family, tribe, or nation. His concern today is for the personal salvation of people of all nations. People do not live in an ideal God-ruled and God-regulated world like

Israel of old or the nations and kingdoms under Christ's rule after his return. They are living in a sinful world under Satan's evil influence. God knows this and is, as we will see, agreeable to modifying the national and ceremonial ideal while at the same time retaining and even expanding the character ideal.

After Christ's return, and at a time when Satan is restrained from influencing humanity (Rev. 20:1-5), we look for a time when Jesus Christ will be worshiped and honored as King of kings and Lord of lords. That will be an ideal time when "the kingdoms of this world have become the kingdoms of our Lord and of His Christ, and He shall reign forever and ever!" (Rev. 11:15).

It is not hard to imagine that all the laws of God that are still relevant and binding will be in full force and effect and required of all nations in those matchless circumstances. The law, if we understand prophecy correctly, and if it is to be taken literally, may very well be in the full "on" position and better and more perfectly fulfilled than at any other time in human history. God may also reinstitute many national and ceremonial functions of his law at that time. The nation of Israel is prophesied to be restored to its former power and glory. It will be an ideal, utopian era.

But as we all know, the ideal often conflicts with the real. I readily see how God would have required the Mosaic food and day regulations of a native-born Israelite in the times of Moses, Samuel, David, or Nehemiah. But would he have expected the same thing of a Gentile Christian slave in the days of Peter and Paul? The Israelite's entire calendar would have revolved around God's holy days, and his circumstances were nearly ideal for keeping those days, but what days could Christian slaves in the Roman Empire regularly "take off" for religious worship and rest? And what special, kosher foods would their masters provide for them?

It's not hard to see why God would require all nations to keep his feast days in what we traditionally called "The Wonderful World Tomorrow," but what about Cornelius, the Roman centurion, one of the first Gentiles converts to Christianity? What days could he arrange to take off from his duties in the Roman army? Could he have gotten two weeks off in the fall every year to go up to Jerusalem for the Feast of Tabernacles?

And what about the Phillippian jailer of Acts 16? How much about the sacred calendar do you think Paul had time to tell him about on the dramatic night of his baptism? What days did he know about and keep before baptism? And if he still had a job at the jail after his conversion, what days did he get off?

My point is that the world of slaves and soldiers and jailers is not an ideal world in which special food and special days are easily arranged. Those people all lived in what Paul called "this present evil world" (Gal.1:4), and their circumstances were far from ideal. They hardly could have been expected to perform all the national and ceremonial requirements of the law, yet they all were Christians who could and did put on the character ideal of Jesus Christ in spite of their less-than-ideal circumstances.

Many New Testament passages define God's character ideal. The fruit of the Spirit found in Galatians 5:22-23 is certainly one such passage, "But the fruit of the Spirit is love, joy, peace, longsuffering, kindness, goodness, faithfulness, gentleness, self-control." But we find no mention here of tithing, sabbath keeping, holy day observance or avoiding unclean meats. Why not?

The same could be asked about I Corinthians 6:9-10 in which Paul lists attitudes and behaviors deemed unacceptable and forbidden for the kingdom of God, yet there is no mention of dietary regulations or sacred days. Again, *why not*? The godly character ideal with its *exceedingly high moral standard* is ever before us in the New Testament, but the national/ceremonial ideal seems to drop out entirely. Emphasis on foods and days is notably absent from all such character ideal prescriptions. We find many truly eternal moral laws and principles, but no ceremonial practices included in the character ideal. As I explained in the previous chapter, that silence should tell us something.

It becomes evident from a study of the New Testament that the godly character ideal can be realized by Christ in us even apart from the national and ceremonial ideal required of Israel through the law of Moses. Surprisingly, it seems that God's highest purpose for us as Christians today is best served when the national/ceremonial law is in the "off" position.

And the reverse of that also seems to be true: God's highest purpose, in terms of attaining the character ideal, did not seem best served when the national/ceremonial law was in the full "on" position. In fact, strict and rigid adherence to the national/ceremonial ideal seemed, somehow, to sidetrack the Israelites from pursuing the character ideal.

We know, for example, that the Jews, as well as many Jewish Christians of the first century, were "all zealous of the law" (Acts 21:20). Many modern commentators understand how the Jews used and interpreted the law to support their belief in themselves as a nation of special status and importance. For example, Alan Segal writes in Paul the Convert,

Pious Jews insisted on circumcision
for all Jewish males, most on the eighth day,
as well as circumcision for all male converts to the religion. Jews also stood out
from their neighbors because of their special rules of resting on the Sabbath. Further, they followed special dietary laws that
affected the food they ate and the way it
was prepared. These facts were noticed by
others....

The laws functioned socially to
mark Jewish identity for those both inside
and outside the community.[1]

The ceremonial laws were high profile identity
markers for the Jews which sharply defined their national
and spiritual identity.

Dunn also is well acquainted with this identifying
function the law fulfilled for the Jews. He notes that "to
be a Jew was to be a member of the covenant, was to observe circumcision, food laws and the sabbath."[2]   He
explains that,

Paul saw...that the covenant is no
longer to be identified or characterized by
such distinctively Jewish observances as
circumcision, food laws and sabbath.
Covenant works had become too closely
identified as *Jewish* observances, *covenant*
righteousness as *national* righteousness
(emphasis his). But to maintain such
identifications was to ignore both the way
the covenant began and the purpose it had
been intended to fulfill.[3]

Dunn observes that this nationalistic and racial interpretation of the law and the covenant "had become a badge not of Abraham's faith but of Israel's boast."[4] His comments remind us of Paul's thought in Romans 2:17, "Indeed you are called a Jew, and rest on the law, and make your boast in God."

Dunn also calls circumcision, the food laws and the sabbath festivals "the clearest identity- and boundary-markers of Judaism as a whole."[5]

But the problem with this blend of zealous nationalism and dogmatic legalism is that by the time of Christ, the national ideal of Israel was in unyielding conflict with the godly character ideal. The badge had become the boast. The boundary had become the barrier. And the celebrated signs had become symptoms of Jewish self-importance and their scorn of other nations.

The clash of the national versus the character ideal is nowhere more apparent than in the many "sabbath incidents" recorded in the Gospels where staunch defenders of the law accused the Son of God of being a sinner and a sabbath breaker. These zealots were so narrowly focused on the ceremonial ideal—matters Paul later would call "shadows"—that they could not see the fullness of the godly character ideal before their eyes in the person of Jesus Christ. Their zeal for God and his law had evolved into a merciless, clannish, and fanatical legalism. Their righteousness was a proud and disdainful self-righteousness.

These fiery zealots had all the right badges, signs, and boundary markers but evidenced little of the love and compassion God wants formed in his people. Their priorities were all wrong. Jesus had to tell them to put the weightier matters of mercy, faith, and justice ahead of tithing mint leaves (Matt.23:23). Paul identifies their problem in Romans 10:2-4,

"For I bear them witness that they have a zeal for God, but not according to knowledge. For they being ignorant of God's righteousness, and seeking to establish their own righteousness, have not submitted to the righteousness of God. For Christ is the end of the law for righteousness to everyone who believes."

A reference that sticks with me in this regard is Dunn's description of the whole Jewish way of life as having an "over-defined character" and an "absorption in details."[6]   I know from experience how deceptively easy it is to over-define the ceremonial ideal and to get bogged down in its many details.

I can't help but apply those comments to our own experience in the Worldwide Church of God. We, too, adopted, then vigorously promoted and staunchly defended the national and ceremonial ideals. We made much of modern Israel's *national* identity and applied the same identifying signs (such as the sabbath, holy days and clean and unclean meats) to "the one and only true church." We, too, were preoccupied with badges, signs, and markers and interpreted them to confirm our special status.

It is not hard for me now to see why the living Christ has mandated change for the Worldwide Church of God. For us in modern times, just as for Israel of old, adopting so many of the national and ceremonial notions of the law of Moses undermined attaining the fullness of the character ideal found in Jesus Christ. Thankfully, we have accepted his correction and have set our priorities straight. We seek today, not to be *special* Christians, but *real* Christians.

In conclusion, let me simply summarize my case in just three points:

1. The law of Moses is no longer required of Christians.

2. The food laws and sacred day laws are part of the law of Moses.

3. Therefore, the food and day laws are now matters of conscience and are no longer binding on Christians as matters of obligation.

Besides offering many chapters of evidence in support of the above points, I have also offered abundant proof that in the New Testament both of these matters were always *administered* as matters of conscience, not as matters of obligation. Paul clearly summed up the early church's administrative position in Romans 14:5, "One man considers one day more sacred than another, another man considers every day alike. *Each one should be fully convinced in his own mind*" (NIV).

I have called to the reader's attention that this was the best administrative policy for the first century Christian church and remains so today. To its credit, the Worldwide Church of God has adopted the Biblical teaching and policy that no longer finds it warring with itself and others on matters of conscience. It is a policy that promotes peace and preserves unity, a policy we can live with.

An Appeal for Reconciliation

And now in closing, I have a brief, special message for those who have left our fellowship, particularly those who, for whatever reason, are now attending no church at all. In the spirit of Isaiah 1:18, I say, "Come, let us reason together."

I think I can understand your hurt, your confusion, your pain. Believe me, I have been through that, too. But I must candidly ask you about your reasons for departing. Did you leave in haste? Did you leave in anger? Did you leave because of your hurt and pain? Or were you simply exhausted by the conflict and confusion you were feeling?

Were your reasons for leaving spiritually mature? Were they well thought out? Were they guided by God, His Spirit and His Word? Or were they perhaps overly influenced by what other people were doing?

If you are no longer attending church anywhere, do you ever think about Hebrews 10:25—"not forsaking the assembly of ourselves together"? Please give these matters some deep thought and prayer.

May I say that I think your place is here—here in the same fellowship of which you have always been a part. Your place is with us, your brethren, your spiritual family. We are not the same without you. Please come back to that part of the body into which you were called.

Fellowship is a peculiar thing. It doesn't always seem to translate easily from one group to another. For a lot of reasons, you make sense here more than anywhere else. You can be understood here better than anywhere else, and you can understand others better who have had the same experiences. We have had a unique history and common experience of trials, faith and growth. We will also share a unique future together.

Come back. Be with us once again. There is no good reason for us to be separated and divided. We need each other, and we could once again live in unity and peace.

Come back. Join with us again in the love and friendship we had before. Let us experience Christ's healing, reconciliation, and renewal.

Come back. With God's help, put your hurt and pain and anger aside, and let us once again go forward together.

Footnotes and References

Introduction
1. Kuhn, Thomas S., The Structure of Scientific Revolutions, Second Edition, 1962/1970, p.76
2. Ibid., p. 68
3. Ibid., p. 147
4. Ibid., pp. 82-83
5. Ibid., 158
6. Ibid.
7. Ibid., p. 159

Chapter One
1. Lenski, R.C.H., The Interpretation of the Acts of the Apostles, 1961, p.591
2. Ibid., p. 599
3. Kistemaker, Simon J., New Testament Commentary, Exposition of Acts of the Apostles, 1990, p. 538
4. Ibid., p. 541
5. Lenski, ibid., p. 592-593
6. Ibid., p. 593
7. Dunn, James D.G., The Theology of Paul's Letter to the Galatians, 1993,   p. 99

Chapter Two
1. The Seventh-day Adventist Bible Commentary, Volume 6, 1980, p.307

Chapter Three
1. Armstrong, Herbert W., "Is ALL Animal Flesh Good Food?", The Plain Truth, February, 1958, p.10
2. Ibid., pp.9-10

3. Ibid., p.10
4. Ibid.
5. Ibid.
6. Ibid., p. 24
7. Ibid.

Chapter Four
1. Kistemaker, Simon J., <u>New Testament Commentary, Exposition of the Acts of the Apostles</u>, 1990, p. 546
2. Lenski, R.C.H., <u>The Interpretation of the Acts of the Apostles</u>, 1961, p. 604

Chapter Five
1. Kistemaker, Simon J., <u>New Testament Commentary, Exposition of the Acts of the Apostles, 1990</u>, p. 380
2. Ibid.
3. Bruce, F. F., <u>The Book of Acts</u>, Revised Edition, 1988, p.285
4. Kistemaker, ibid., p. 387

Chapter Six
1. Bruce, F. F., <u>The Book of Acts</u>, Revised Edition, 1988, p. 295
2. Kistemaker, Simon J., <u>New Testament Commentary, Expostion of the Acts of the Apostles</u>, 1990, p. 555
3. Lenski, R.C.H., <u>The Interpretation of the Acts of The Apostles</u>, 1961, p. 616
4. Kistemaker, ibid., p. 555-556

Chapter Seven
1. Maccoby, Hyam, <u>The Mythmaker</u>, 1987, p. 148

Chapter Eight
1. Armstrong, Herbert W., <u>Pagan Holidays—or God's Holy Days—Which?</u>, pp. 10-11
2. Ibid.
3. Ibid.
4. Ibid., p. 12
5. Ibid.
6. Ibid.

Chapter Ten
1. Armstrong, Herbert W., <u>Pagan Holidays—or God's Holy Days—Which?</u>, pp. 11-12
2. Ibid.
3. "Does It Matter What Days We Observe?", <u>The Good News</u>, September, 1960, p. 4
4. Ibid., p. 6
5. "The Colossian Heresy", <u>The Good News</u>, July-August, 1989, p. 27
6. Ibid.
7. Ibid.

Chapter Eleven
1. Guthrie, Donald, <u>New Testament Introduction</u>, 1968, pp. 685-698
2. <u>The Broadman Commentary</u>, 1971, p. 239
3. <u>What Is Your Destiny?</u>, United Church of God, 1996, p. 9
4. <u>The Expositor's Bible Commentary</u>, Volume 11, 1980, p. 204

Chapter Thirteen
1. Dunn, James D.G., <u>Word Biblical Commentary</u>, Volume 38, Romans 9-16, Section G, "The Particular Problem of Food Laws and Holy Days," p. 800

2. Ibid.
3. Ibid., p. 801
4. Ibid., p. 806
5. Turner, George A., <u>The Wesleyan Bible Commentary</u>, Volume Five,   pp. 85-86
6. Bruce, F.F., <u>The Epistles to the Colossians, to Philemon, and to the Ephesians</u>, 1984, p. 114

Chapter Fourteen
1. <u>The Seventh-day Adventist Bible Commentary</u>, Volume 7, p. 206
2. Ibid.
3. Armstrong, Herbert W., <u>Which Day Is the Sabbath of the New Testament?</u>, pp. 13-14

Chapter Fifteen
1. Segal, Alan F., <u>Paul the Convert</u>, 1990, p.193
2. Dunn, James D.G., <u>Jesus, Paul, and the Law</u>, 1990, p. 194
3. Ibid., p. 197
4. Ibid., p. 202
5. Ibid., p. 243
6. Dunn, James D.G., <u>The Theology of Paul's Letter to the Galatians</u>, 1993,   p. 98

Bibliography

Armstrong, Herbert W. "Is ALL Animal Flesh Good Food?", The Plain Truth, February, 1958

Armstrong, Herbert W., Pagan Holidays—or God's Holy Days—Which?

Armstrong, Herbert W., Which Day Is the Sabbath of the New Testament?

Bruce, F. F. The Book of Acts, Revised Edition (Grand Rapids:Eerdmans, 1988)

Bruce, F.F. The Epistles to the Colossians, to Philemon, and to the Ephesians (Grand Rapids: Eerdmans, 1984)

Dunn, James D.G. Jesus, Paul, and the Law Louisville:Westminster/John Knox Press, 1990)

Dunn, James D.G. The Theology of Paul's Letter to the Galatians (Cambridge: Cambridge University Press, 1993)

Dunn, James D.G. Word Biblical Commentary, Volume 38, Romans 9-16 (Dallas: Word Books, 1988)

Guthrie, Donald. New Testament Introduction (Downers Grove: Inter-Varsity Press, 1970)

Kistemaker, Simon J. New Testament Commentary,
    Exposition of Acts of the Apostles (Grand
    Rapids: Baker House, 1990)

Kuhn, Thomas S. The Structure of Scientific Revolutions,
    Second Edition (Chicago: University of Chicago
    Press, 1962,1970)

Lenski, R.C.H. The Interpretation of the Acts of the
    Apostles (Minneapolis: Augsburg Publishing
    House, 1961)

Maccoby, Hyam. The Mythmaker (San Francisco:
Harper Collins,1987)

Turner, George A. The Wesleyan Bible Commentary,
    Volume Five, Philippians and Colossians
    (Grand Rapids: Eerdmans, 1965)

Segal, Alan F. Paul the Convert (New Haven: Yale
    University Press,1990)

Index

Administrative policy,
156-158, 188
Arguments from silence,
174-177
Armstrong, Garner Ted,
14
Armstrong, Herbert W.,
11, 14, 16, 37, 45-52,
69, 84-92, 95, 109-113
Atonement, Day of,
129-130

Basic law,
46
Bereans,
33
Blood,
74, 78

Ceremonial law,
181-183
Character ideal,
179-183
Circumcision,
33-35, 137, 139-140,
180
Clean and unclean,
39, 44, 48, 62-64, 80
Commandments,
41, 99-100

Cornelius,
61-62
Covenant,
92-93

Essenes,
136
Eucharist,
100

Fabrics, mixed,
38, 97
Fasting days,
145-147, 154
Festivals,
41, 83-94
Fellowship,
72, 75, 189

Galatians,
135-143
Gentiles,
54-58, 68, 73, 148-152
Good News magazine,
113, 115
"Good things to come,"
128-131

Health laws,
46-49, 79

Holy Days,
25, 39, 84, 85, 88, 90

Identity markers,
185-186

James,
71-76
Jerusalem Conference,
32-33, 37, 39, 53,
77-78, 81
Jews,
31-36, 53, 61, 65-66,
81-82, 151-153
Judaism,
35, 137, 186

Kosher,
39-40, 79

Law of Moses,
11, 33-36, 37-44,
82-94, 187-188
Land sabbath,
38, 95
Leap Year,
83
Legalism,
17, 32, 37, 57, 74, 145,
159, 186
Lord's Supper,
100

Millennial reign,
179
Moses,
90-92
Moral law,
171-174

National ideal,
151-187
Nero,
81
New Moons,
101-102, 106-107, 110,
116, 129-130, 134

Passover,
100, 128
Pagan days,
135-136, 140-141
Peter,
53-58
Pentecost,
61, 83
Pharisees,
35
Physical laws,
46-49
Physical sin,
46
Plain Truth,
13, 16, 45

Prophecy,
17, 101-103

Reconciliation,
188-190
Rituals,
86-87
Romans,
145-160

Sabbath,
11, 25, 39, 163-178
Sacrifices,
39, 44, 129
Sermon on the Mount,
100
Shadow,
112-116, 120-125
Slaves,
183
Substance,
120, 124

Table fellowship,
75
Tabernacles,
11, 83, 99, 102-103,
127, 133
Ten Commandments,
99, 167-170
Tithing,
11, 95, 98

Tkach, Joseph W.,
14-17, 27, 28
Tkach, Joseph (Jr,),
17
Trumpets,
83, 132

Unclean foods,
48-49, 62, 69
Unleavened Bread,
83

Vegetarianism,
147, 153-156

Worldwide Church of God,
11, 18, 21, 29-31, 58
World Tomorrow,
102, 183
World Tomorrow telecast,
14, 15

Yoke,
56-57, 69, 139

Notes

Notes

About the author

David Albert

David Albert is an evangelist in the Worldwide Church of God and former presenter on The World Tomorrow telecast. During most of his nearly 35-year ministry he has taught at Ambassador University. He holds a Ph.D. in Counseling Psychology from the University of Oregon (1981) and currently serves as Professor of Psychology. He and his wife Simone reside in Big Sandy, Texas. Dr. Albert is an avid bridge player and wooden boat builder.

To purchase a copy of "Difficult Scriptures" from the publisher, send your prepaid order to the address below. Enclose check or money order for $14.95 U.S. ($16.95 Canada and outside the U.S.A., Texas residents add $1.05 sales tax). Include $2 for shipping and handling. Allow 2-3 weeks for delivery.

Send your order to:
Tyler House
Box 132327
Tyler, Texas 75713